INDEX

OF

BALTIMORE

COUNTY

MARYLAND

WILLS

1659-1850

Bettie S. Carothers and Robert W. Barnes

HERITAGE BOOKS

2011

HERITAGE BOOKS
AN IMPRINT OF HERITAGE BOOKS, INC.

Books, CDs, and more—Worldwide

For our listing of thousands of titles see our website
at
www.HeritageBooks.com

Published 2011 by
HERITAGE BOOKS, INC.
Publishing Division
100 Railroad Ave. #104
Westminster, Maryland 21157

International Standard Book Numbers
Paperbound: 978-0-7884-3482-2
Clothbound: 978-0-7884-8788-0

CONTENTS

INTRODUCTION

This index was compiled using several sources: the index of wills at the Baltimore City Court House, a partial index to the wills compiled by the late Annie Walker Burns, the original will books at the Hall of Records in Annapolis, and the abstracts of Will Books, numbers 4 through 23, compiled by Mrs. Burns at the Maryland Historical Society.

It was found that in some cases Mrs. Burns' will abstracts contained wills not in the court house index. A check of the original will books revealed that the wills did in fact exist on the pages cited by Mrs. Burns. The court house index and Mrs. Burns' index follow the Burr Index Form, with names arranged by the first three letters; e.g., Thompson, Thomsen, and Thomas are all listed together.

The advantages of this index over the court house index and Mrs. Burns partial index are first, that the entries in this index are in alphabetical order, second, that every effort has been made to mistakes in spelling made by the compilers of the court house index, and third, this index contains wills not indexed at the court house.

Where a question exists as to the spelling of a name, the name has been entered under two or more spellings. Some wills had two page references. The second page may refer to a codicil or to the renunciation of the will by a widow or administratrix, or executrix.

Persons desiring photocopies of the wills should write to the Hall of Records in Annapolis.

Following this introduction is a list of additional wills found m too late to be included in the main part of the text.

The entries in the text contain the name of the testator, the year the will was probated, and the book and page number on which the will can be found.

The compilers wish to thank Mrs. Mary K. Meyer of the Maryland Hiztorical Society and the staff of the Register of Wills Office in Baltimore City for their help and cooperation.

Bettie S. Carothers
Robert Barnes

ADDITIONAL WILLS

ACKERMAN, Christiona	1789	4-344
BROOKHART, Martha	1840	17-456
BUDD, George	1787	4-230
COATES, William	1781	3-421
D'ARCY, John H.	1835	15-390
FISHER, George	1799	6-182
FOWBLE, Peter	1799	6-210
GOLDSBOROUGH, John	1825	12- 85
GONGES, Arnand	1797	6- 50
IVES, James	1704	1- 68
McCOVE, Thomas	1767	3- 69
MILLAIN, Henry	1737	1-293
PROEBSTING, Theodore Conrad		
	1821	11-313
St.CLAIR, James	1761	2-341
William	1825	12-188

ST. JOHNS, Christopher	1835	15-365
STANSIFORD, Henry	1815	10- 59
STILES, George	1819	11- 12
SWEENY, Paul	1844	20- 41
SWITZER, John	1848	22-142
THOMSON, Mary	1803	7-234
TIPTON, Joshua	1831	14- 45
TODES, John Yost	1837	16-244
VIBRANS, William	1833	14-285
WALTERS, Alexander,		
of Samuel	1835	15-415
John Henry	1839	17-426
WANTLAND, Thomas	1816	10-226
WANTON, Rose	1847	22-48
WARFIELD, Elijah	1818	9-531
WATSON, Rachel	1835	15-224
WATTS, Signey	1836	16-162
WEEMS, Augusta	1837	16-243
Charles H.	1821	11-281
WILKER, John	1774	3-290
WILLIAMS, Eliza	1831	14- 60
WILLSON, Henrietta	1831	14- 25
WILLSON, James	1776	3-586
William	1787	4-244

INDEX TO BALTIMORE COUNTY WILLS

INDEX OF BALTIMORE COUNTY WILLS

ANDERS, George	1810	8-506
ANDERSON, Benjamin	1803	7-205
Charles	1740	1-328
Edward	1846	21-291
Ellen	1834	15-442
Hugh	1837	16-228
James	1824	12-43&1
James	1765	3- 40
John	1803	7-141
John	1711	1 -93
John	1820	11-130
Joseph	1789	4-352 & 372
Robert	1789	4-372
Sarah	1812	9-245
Theodore	1840	18- 30
William	1775	3-310
William	1835	15-424
ANDREW, Abraham	1784	4- 11
Littlewood	1835	15-321
ANDREWS, Ephraim	1784	3-591
Nathaniel	1699	1-183
Susanne	1817	10-307
Thomas	1784	3-572
William	1784	3-583
ANGEL, Maria C.	1826	12-294
ANKER, Hillel	1841	18-410
ANSPACK, John	1823	11-621
ANTHONY, Henry	1849	23-217
APPLEMAN, Conrad	1818	10-515
ARDEN, John	1694	1-101
ARDREY, Alexander	1827	12-382
RRES, Charlotte Waltham	1834	14-440
ARGUIT, Eli	1844	20-208
ARLOW, William	1837	16-305
ARMACOST, Michael	1840	18- 63
ARMIGER, Thomas	1676	1-112
ARMITAGE, Ann	1835	15-360
James	1815	10-45
Rachel	1822	11-470
ARMSTRONG, Francis,	1837	16-209
Frank	1816	10-148
James	1839	17-310
James	1823	11-503
John	1832	14-260
Mary	1848	22-280
Peter	1837	16-185
Solomon	1749	1-465
Thomas	1824	12- 56
Thomas	1841	18-391

ARNENT, Ann	1828	13-137
ARNOLD, Anthony	1721	1-508
David	1780	3-394
Elizabeth	1771	3-196
John	1807	8-273
John	1842	19-116
Joseph	1826	12-259
Peter	1813	9-344 & 387
Peter	1842	19- 38
Rebecca	1788	4-316
Susanna	1708	1-103
ARTHUR, Damaris	1818	10-507
Lucy	1848	22-255
ASBURNER, John	1783	3-488
ASBURY, Francis	1816	10-172
ASH, Mary Anne	1765	3- 41
ASHBOW, Henry	1798	6-100
John	1826	12-229
ASHWELL, William	1806	8- 57
ASHER, Anthony	1764	2-184
Anthony	1828	12- 86
Barnet	1816	10-107
Mary	1804	7-338
ASHLEY, Millicent	1845	20-458 & 494
ASHMAN, George	1699	1- 43
ASPY, William	1798	6-147
ATHERTON, James	1779	3-381
William	1821	11-259
ATHEY, Walter	1821	11-265
ATKERSON, Joseph	1800	6-257
ATKINSON, Anne	1823	11-573
Anthony	1811	9-182
George	1811	9-167
Isaac	1829	13-222
John	1754	2- 58
John	1806	8- 38
John	1842	18-485
Sarah	1849	23- 45
AUGHARD, John	1748	1-427
AUSTINE, Christopher	1818	10-425
AUSTIN, Charles C.	1849	23- 89
Gabriel	1796	5-369
AUKERMAN, George	1780	3-408
AUZOLLE, John B.	1839	17-235
AVIS, Jarvis	1804	7-340
AVISE, Charles	1825	12-154
AVISSE, Victorie	1833	14-298

BACKER, Charles	1790	4-394
Providence	1846	21-312
BACON, Martin	1785	4-106
BACCHUS, Kitty	1818	10-514
BACCKER, John W. F.	1842	19-177
BACON, Martin	1785	4-106
BAGFORD, Wm.	1823	11-539
BAGNALL, Henry S.	1847	21-477
		& 496
BAILEY, Enoch	1766	3- 45
George	1754	2- 56
Hellin	1801	6-405
Jabez	1769	3-107
James	1848	22-445
John	1801	6-406
Samuel	1774	3-295
Thomas	1795	5-316
William	1801	6-396
BAILLIE, John	1812	9-276
BAIR, Ann	1812	9-275
BAKER, Anna	1841	18-435
Benjamin	1805	7-384
Betsey A.	1832	11-265
George	1844	20- 85
		& 138
John M.	1796	5-406
John	1807	8-214
John S.	1843	19-392
Joseph	1799	6-165
Lloyd G.	1845	20-441
Mary	1849	23- 14
Mathias	1799	6-221
Maurice	1827	12-359
Nicholas	1799	6-212
Samuel	1835	15-402
Sahah (sic)	1835	15-359
Sarah	1846	21-207
Thomas	1835	15-414
William	1817	10-288
BALDERSTON, Isaiah	1817	10-357
BALDWIN, Abraham	1843	19-334
BALE, Anthony	1720	3- 2
BALE, Thomas	1707	1- 97
Urath	1708	1-102
BALEY, Thomas	1771	3-183
BALL, Sarah	1829	13-168
William	1686	1-65
BALTZELL, Jacob	1850	23-468
BANDEL, John	1828	13- 45
BANKHARD, Levace	1819	11- 45

BANKSON, Joseph	1762	2-137
BANTON, Charles	1821	11-274
BARBER, Margaret	1822	11-453
Thomas	1799	6-228
BARBIE, Alexander	1822	11-357
Antonie	1822	11-346
BARCALAY, William	1814	9-392
		& 458
BARETT, John	1717	1-149
BAREY, Susanna	1835	15-396
BARGE, Andrew	1830	13-467
BARHAM, John	1817	10-305
BARKER, John	1707	1- 18
Morris	1762	2-153
Priscella	1847	21-449
William	1822	11-500
BARKEWITCH, Charlotta	1837	16-404
BARKMAN, John	1821	11-303
BARLING, Aaron	1800	6-309
Sarah	1835	15-302
BARLOW, James, Jr.	1721	2- 5
James	1721	1-512
BARNADY, Elias	1812	9-252
BARNARD, John	1803	7-192
BARNHART, David	1827	12-334
John	1841	18-270
BARNES, Adam	1809	8-416
Dennis	1831	14- 57
Ford	1825	12-215
John	1823	11-582
John	1834	14-446
Mahala	1804	7-314
Mary A.	1844	20- 5
Robson	1804	7-263
Whiteley	1814	9-464
William P.	1827	12-407
BARNETT, Andrew	1793	5-131
Catherine	1794	5-147
BARNEY, John H.	1840	17-494
Joshua	1819	10-543
Louis	1850	23-425
William	1746	1-370
BARNEYT, Daniel	1780	3-399
BARNS, Ford	1749	1-423
Ford	1761	2-325
BARNUM, David	1844	20- 62
BARRELL, Colborn	1810	8-517
BARRETT, Patricia	1836	16-129
BARRICK, Emeline	1845	20-462
BARRICKMAN, Hannah	1846	21-239

BARRICKMAN, Joseph	1811	9-125		BAYZAND, Susanna	1808	8-325
BARROLL, James	1845	20-231		BEALE, Evan	1821	11-282
BARRON, James B.	1831	14- 73		BEALL, Asenath G.	1845	20-487
Mary	1844	20-186		BEALMER, Francis	1834	15-127
Nathan (Barrow)	1846	21-231		BEAM, George	1815	10- 18
BARROW, Elizabeth	1793	5- 98		George	1829	13-217
John	1780	3-405		Sarah	1817	10-392
BARRY, Elizabeth	1835	15-226		Sidney	1826	12-272
Lawrence	1813	9-304		BEAMER, Philip	1843	19-249
BARTON, Ann	1816	10-186		BEARD, Elizabeth	1846	21-206
Asel	1823	11-615		George A.	1774	3-294
James	1734	2-205		James	1843	19-319
James	1774	2-272		Rebecca S.	1847	22-101
James	1831	14- 61		BEARGUPILE, Jacob	1821	11-223
John	1784	4- 19		BEASLEY, James	1815	10- 38
Seth	1814	9-456		BEASMAN, Joseph	1817	10-368
Thomas	1730	1-245		Joseph	1738	1-295
Thomas	1841	18-299		Rachel	1824	12- 35
BASSETT, Isaac	1809	8-452		Thomas	1824	11-653
BASTIAN, John B.	1838	17-165		Thomas	1833	14-294
BATEMAN, Amzi	1816	10-196		William	1769	3-112
BATHNIST, Matthew	1847	22-37		William	1827	12-427
BATTEE, Ferdinand	1808	8-381		BEATTY, Charles	1804	7-336'
John	1800	6-259		BEAUER, John	1815	9-514
Richard H.	1848	22-352		BEAVER, Martin	1832	14-196
BATTIE, Ferdinando	1783	3-528		Susanna	1824	12- 11
BAUER, David	1844	20-135		BECK, Charles	1770	3-139
Michael	1848	22-335		BECKLEY, Elizabeth	1824	2- 12
BAUGHMAN, Frederick	1848	22-425		Henry	1816	10-220
Jacob	1838	17-134		BEDENHAM, Bernard	1840	18- 59
BAUMAN, Melchoir	1848	22-351		BEDFORD, Benjamin	1830	13-354
BAUMEISTER, Henry	1845	20-400		BEDINGER, Daniel	1839	17-224
BAUSMAN, Lawrence	1797	6- 32		BEDISON, Thomas	1801	6-401
John	1838	16-436		BEEHLER, Gotlib	1848	22-184
BAXLEY, George	1848	22-464		BEEMAN, Joseph	1773	3-269
Mary	1804	7-307		BEERS, Thomas	1850	23-452
BAXTER, Edmund	1774	3-297		BEESTON, Rev. Francis	1809	8-466
Eleanor	1813	9-316		BEETLE, Elizabeth	1796	5-405
James	1807	8-266		BEGODIS, Cornelius	1807	8-234
John	1757	2-230		BEHO, Moses	1835	15-298
John H.	1846	21- 97		Nancy	1835	15-404
Mary	1808	8-319		BELL, Eve	1812	9-270
Sarah	1843	19-253		Hugh	1837	16-202
BAY, William	1773	3-262		Jane	1836	16- 40
BAYLEY, Henry E.	1823	11-509		John	1826	12-289
BAYLIS, Jane	1847	22-109		Beniah/Peniah	1848	22-242
Samuel	1773	3-276		William	1781	3-436
BAYLY, George	1821	11-220		William	1846	21-197
Margaret	1848	22-239		BELLI, Seraphine	1812	9-220
Mary A.	1847	21-420		BELOW, Thomas	1744	2- 24

BLACKISTON, George M.	1814	9-427	John W.	1819	11- 11
BLADEN, Thomas,	1783	4-207	Joshua	1768	3- 81
BLADDGET, Otis	1845	20-263	Luke	1773	3-255
BLAKE, James	1848	22-138	Martha	1814	9-441
William	1836	16-67	Nichodemus	1804	7-315
BLANCHARD, John G.	1834	15-142	Peter	1705	1- 65
BLAMEY, Thomas	1785	4- 67	Peter	1718	1-182
BLEAHY, Thomas	1785	4- 67	Peter	1763	2-358
BLIZZARD, Asa	1846	21-135	Peter	1769	3-106
William	1810	8-496	Peter	1821	11-332
William	1816	10-254	Phineas	1818	10-445
BLODGETT, Otis	1845	20-263	Richard	1763	2-360
BLOODGOOD, John	1811	9- 94	Samuel	1796	5-366
BLOOM, John	1816	10-150	Sarah	1770	3-140
BLUFFORD, Jonathan	1832	14-203	Thomas	1756	2- 91
BOARD, James	1763	2-362	William	1769	3-104
Jonathan	1806	8-110	BONDEREAN, Catherine	1828	13- 79
BOBBITS, Charles	1799	6-225	BONINGER, Gustav	1848	22-386
BOBLETTS, Elizabeth	1817	10-184	BONNEFIN, Nicholas	1838	17- 74
BOBLETS, John	1822	11-412	BONNET, Joseph	1832	14-174
Stople	1831	14- 47	BOMSTED, James	1802	7- 62
BODDY, Stephen	1742	1-336	BOODY, John J.	1844	20- 37
BODEROTH, Charles	1811	9-129	BOOKER, Lambert	1813	9-388
BODLEY, Thomas	1811	9-179			& 396
BOERING, James	1819	11-364	BOOKHULTZ, Joseph	1848	22-456
BOISSEAU, David W.	1823	12-532	BOONE, John B. R. C.	1824	11-634
BOLE, Jane	1812	9-252	Richard	1784	3-559
BOLENDER, Johannes	1849	23-127	Robert	1848	22-299
BOLES, George	1797	5-518	Sarah	1807	8-156
BOLING, Luraney	1844	20-148	Thomas	1775	3-307
BOLLINGER, Anne	1834	15-183	William G.	1782	3-471
Joseph	1826	12-319	BOOTH, Don A.	1849	23-237
BOLLMAN, Thomas	1819	11-597	Elizabeth	1839	17- 38
BOLTE, Henry	1829	13-233	Margaret	1833	14-373
John F.	1845	20-409	William	1818	10-454
BOLTON, John	1839	17-387	BOOTHBY, Edward	1698	1-171
Henry	1818	10-510	BORDLEY, John B.	1808	8-300
Margaret H.	1829	13-331	BOREING, John	1690	1- 85
BOND, Ann	1743	1-351			& 86
Benjamin	1848	22-189	Joshua	1822	11-408
Charles	1784	3-556	Thomas	1761	2-331
Charles	1810	8-496	BORING, Elizabeth	1785	4-108
Edward	1797	5-497	Josiah	1826	12-292
Eleanor	1838	17- 36	Martha	1813	9-337
Eleanor	1843	19-411	Sarah	1763	2-361
Elizabeth	1787	4-200	Thomas	1795	5-341
Elizabeth	1810	9- 16	William	1811	9-115
James	1809	8-369	BORIS, John	1848	22-171
John	1720	1-169	BORLAND, Thomas	1838	16-441
John	1792	5- 75	BORN, John	1817	10-274
John	1815	10- 4	BORNS, Jacob	1835	15-370

BORNSHEAGEL, John	1848	22-421	Benjamin	1748	1-433
BOS, Fienti	1796	5-416	Benjamin	1770	3-142
BOSCH, John	1850	23-424	Benjamin	1814	9- 49
BOSE, Catherine	1839	17-178			& 415
Jacob	1797	6- 38	Catherine	1835	15-231
BOSS, Adam	1839	17-346	Edward	1847	21-368
John	1840	18-140	James	1800	6-276
BOSLEY, Ann	1828	13-151	John	1742	1-333
Ann	1833	14-332	John	1748	1-443
Ann, Jr.	1837	16-293	Jonas	1699	1- 39
Caleb	1835	15-235	Jonas	1728	2-194
Charles	1762	2-131	Jonas	1751	3-413
Daniel	1827	12-403	Joshua	1815	10- 78
Elijah	1841	18-356	Josias	1793	5- 89
Eliza	1842	18-495	Josias	1805	7-444
Elizabeth	1785	4- 62	Martha	1704	1- 89
Gamaliel	1842	19-154	Mary	1762	2-156
Greenbury	1815	9-516	Mary	1789	4-355
		& 525	Mary	1816	10-181
Hannah	1777	3-325	Mary	1822	11-387
Hannah	1816	10-121	Nathan	1770	3-138
James	1843	19-470	Nathan	1810	9- 70
James	1850	23-436	Rees	1769	3-126
Joseph	1776	3-330	Ruth	1836	15-488
Joseph	1780	3-393	Solomon	1804	7-293
Joseph	1835	15-333	Solomon	1833	14-403
John	1772	3-213	Susanna	1827	12-429
Nicholas H.	1847	21-371	BOWER, Eberhard E.	1834	15-103
Philip	1840	17-450	BOWERS, Henry	1825	12-136
Ruth	1792	5- 75	William	1823	11-580
Temperance	1823	11-608	BOWLY, Daniel	1745	2-212
Thomas	1839	17-413	BOWMAN, Jacob	1850	23-495
Walter	1715	1-110	BOWSER, Joseph	1826	12-274
William	1754	2- 59	BOYCE, Benjamin	1810	9- 29
William	1832	14-265	John	1815	10- 40
Zebulon	1791	4-528	Rebecca	1775	3-506
BOSMAN, Edward	1797	6- 16	Roger	1772	3-205
BOSS, Adam	1839	17-346	BOYD, Andrew	1802	6-525
John	1840	18-140	Ann	1833	14-282
BOSSIN, Charles	1812	9-241	Elizabeth	1844	20- 70
BOSTON, Samuel	1676	1- 41	James McH.	1847	22-121
BOSWELL, Joseph	1814	9-425	John	1790	4-404
BOTTRILL, Francis	1841	18-311	William L.	1828	13- 61
BOUNDS, Joseph	1814	9-448	BOYLE, James	1783	3-499
BOURNE, Sylvanus	1819	10-557	BRACKEN, John	1828	13- 29
BOURY, Louis	1819	11- 40	BRADEHOUSE, Conrad	1819	11- 63
BOVINGTON, Henry	1848	22-430	BRADDISH, John	1802	7-115
BOWAN, William	1843	19-346	BRADDOCK, Mary	1781	3-426
BOWDEN, George	1794	5-174	BRADEHOUSE, Conrad	1819	11- 63
BOWEN, Benjamin	1742	1-330	BRADENBAUGH, John H.	1840	18-147

INDEX OF BALTIMORE COUNTY WILLS

BRADFORD, John B.	1814	9-406		BRINKETT, Susannah	1836	16- 30
BRADLEY, Isaac	1844	19-490		William	1834	15- 87
BRADSHAW, Mary	1830	13-458		BRISCOE, Samuel H.	1815	10- 82
Richard	1842	19- 62		BRISTOL, Jane	1842	19-122
BRADY, John	1784	3-492		BRISTOW, David	1838	16-492
John	1816	10-144		BRITENOLDER, Adam	1810	8-469
Patrick	1836	16-22		BRITT, Robert	1793	5-114
BRAGGER, Ann	1821	11-252		BRITTON, John	1826	12-218
BRAMBLE, Nathan	1847	22- 99		BROAD, Barbara	1733	2-285
BRAMMELL, George	1770	3-136		John	1709	1- 27
BRANCHED, Conrad	1804	7-284		BROMWELL, Spedding	1803	7-128
BRAND, Daniel	1831	14- 9		BROOK, Rachel	1807	8-141
BRANAN, Patrick	1814	9-437		BROOKE, Clement	1807	8-238
BRANNAN, John	1840	17-481		BROOKS, Charles	1824	12- 41
John	1846	21- 37		Joseph	1841	18-471
BRANON, Archibald	1766	3- 40		Thomas R.	1834	15-122
BRANDT, William	1815	10- 57		BROTHERS, Henry	1797	5-519
BRANSON, Battis	1841	18-337		BROUST, Conrad	1766	3- 33
Oren	1815	10- 49		BROWN, Abel	1796	5-382
BRANT, Adam	1775	3-287		Abel	1834	14-500
BRANTZ, Lewis	1838	16-457		Alexander	1834	14-488
BRAYTON, Isaac	1805	7-453		Andrew	1823	11-515
BREADY, Thomas	1813	9-367		Ann	1836	16- 65
BREDEMEYER, Frederick	1850	23-328		Charles	1840	17-460
BRENAN, Thomas B., of				David	1807	8-272
Brice	1843	19-211		David	1809	8-384
BRENDEL, Frederick	1815	9-524		Dixon	1774	3-281
Maria C.	1828	13-143		Dorothy	1836	16-159
BRENTON, Richard	1834	15- 81		Elias	1800	6-303
BREREWOOD, Thomas	1746	1 -379		Elizabeth	1825	12-187
		& 382		Elizabeth	1832	14-178
BREVITT, John	1824	12- 45		Elizabeth	1832	14-204
		& 71		Elizabeth	1830	13-338
BREWER, Edward	1840	18- 72		Francis	1741	1-384
Hubbard	1756	2-108		George	1764	2-173
John	1835	15-248		George	1822	11-467
Mary	1835	15-296		George	1845	20-274
BRIAN, Charles	1844	20-115		Grace	1843	19-217
Isaac	1839	17-383		Jacob	1810	2- 9
James	1812	9-287		Jacob F.	1792	5- 35
Nicholas	1830	13-398		James	1795	5-314
BRIANT, Isabella C.	1850	23-346		James	1782	3-484
John	1844	20-130		James	1810	9- 74
BRIARLY, Robert	1764	2-330		James	1811	9- 91
BRICE, James	1765	3- 8		James	1837	16-269
BRIDENBUCK, Valentine	1802	6-538		James S.	1837	16-266
BRIEN, Anne E.	1834	15- 43		Jane	1847	22- 40
Robert C.	1833	14-346		Jehosheba	1829	13-280
BRIENS, Lawrence	1795	5-301		Jesse	1802	7- 55
BRINCE, Henry	1784	4- 27		John	1716	1-230

BROWN, John	1784	4- 30		BRYARLY, Robert	1766	3- 31
John	1791	4-532		BRYMAN, James	1797	6- 22
John	1801	6-377		William	1806	8- 36
John	1802	6-493		BRYSON, John	1832	14-122
John	1810	8-490		BUCHANAN, Andrew	1786	4-120
John	1814	9-469		Archibald	1785	4- 72
John	1823	11-531		Edward	1843	19-380
John	1823	11-565		Eleanor	1758	2- 73
John	1825	12-166		Elizabeth S.	1830	13-446
John	1826	12-320		George	1750	2- 27
John G.	1831	14- 5		George	1810	9- 67
Josiah	1822	11-421		Hannah	1802	7- 9
Lucy	1829	13-195		Hephzibah	1832	14-260
Martha	1786	4-113		James	1783	3-552
Martin	1846	21-163		James	1822	11-412
Mary	1768	3- 93		James A.	1840	18- 25
Mary, alias Mary				James C.	1823	11-561
Dutton	1769	3-129		John L.	1827	12-413
Mary	1836	15-434		Latitia	1846	21-261
Mary A.	1846	21-154		Lloyd	1762	2-124
Moses	1817	10-350		Margaret	19-351	1843
Nancy	1835	15-338		Mary	1733	2-284
Richard	1827	12-330		Sidney	1841	18-231
Ruth	1826	12-276		Susanna	1798	6-131
Samuel	1713	1-190		William, of G.	1825	12- 81
Sarah	1832	14-229		BUCK, Benj.	1808	8-280
Sarah	1803	7-178		Benjamin	1841	18-201
Solomon	1813	9-322		Benjamin	1848	22-427
Stephen	1814	9-508		Christopher	1807	8-150
Thomas	1680	1-52		Dorcas	1824	12- 33
Thomas	1708	1- 19		Jacob	1828	13- 31
Thomas	1766	3- 42		John, of Benjamin	1849	23-249
Thomas	1793	5-102		Joshua	1812	9-217
Thomas	1809	8-462		Kezia	1840	16-477
Thomas	1816	10-214		Susannah	1793	5-132
Thomas	1847	21-350		BUCKEY, Daniel	1847	22-112
Uria	1837	16-410		Elizabeth	1844	19-481
William	1794	5-206		BUCKINGHAM, John	1800	6-328
William	1812	9-238		Sarah	1802	7- 46
William	1828	13- 83		Thomas	1837	16-415
William	1832	14-140		BUCKLER, Humphrey	1832	14-215
BROWNE, William	1829	13-287		BUCKNELL, Thomas	1720	1-162
BROWNESS, William	1798	6- 70		BUJAC, Mathew	1834	14-458
BROWNING, Peregrine G.	1816	10-166		BULL, Abraham	1762	2-154
BRUBECK, Rody	1785	4-101		Christopher	1835	15-298
BRUCE, Charles K.	1829	13-183'		Columbus	1845	20-465
BRUFF, William	1802	7-108		Elizabeth	1847	21-412
BRYAN, Charles	1837	16-340		Hannah	1760	2-276
Frederick	1822	11-492		Jacob	1756	1-477
Lewis	1676	1-107		Jacob	1825	12-111
				Jarrett	1845	20-280

INDEX OF BALTIMORE COUNTY WILLS

BULL, John	1757	2-243	John	1849	23- 58
John	1817	10-286	Maria F.	1848	22-247
Nicholas, Sr.	1846	21- 84	Moses	1847	21-431
William, of Isaac	1830	13-445	Peter	1771	3-184
William, Sr.	1833	14-352	Ruth	1808	8-350
BULLITT, Mary	1839	17-241	Thomas	1780	3-401
BULLUS, Charles	1850	23-370	Thomas	1845	20-450
BUNDY, Ann	1833	14-303	Wm.	1830	13-400
BUNJIE, Robert	1840	17-453	BUTTERWORTH, Isaac	1729	2-191
BUNTEN, Billy D.	1814	9-489	Isaac	1746	1-369
BURCHFIELD, Adam	1766	3- 42	BUTTON, Robert	1803	7-151
BURGAN, Philip	1845	20-455	William	1804	7-285
Thomas	1836	15-457	BYARD, Ephraim	1825	12-168
BURGESS, Catherine S.	1838	17- 41	BYERLY, Catherine	1836	15-463
Hugh	1770	3-134	BYRUS, Thomas	1848	22-328
John	1816	10-169			
Mary	1794	5-156			
BURGOYNE, Hugh	1798	6- 80	CAHILL, James	1832	14-234
BURHAM, Hezekiah	1847	22- 97	Jane	1845	20-447
		159&179	Rosanna	1838	17-159
BURK, Henry	1708	1- 18	CALDER, James	1808	8 -352
James	1802	7- 36	Margaret	1829	13-197
Richard	1842	19-141	CALEBOUGH, Apelona	1822	11-445
Ulrick	1762	2-117	CALEY, Frederick	1781	3-421
BURKE, Barney	1844	20-113	CALHOUN, James	1816	10-199
Charles	1813	9-309	CALLAN, Andrew	1846	21-243
James	1837	16-374	CALMAN, John R.	1769	3-166
BURLAND, James	1825	12-104	Joseph	1802	6-541
BURNESTON, Anna	1842	19- 47	CALTRIDER, George	1831	14- 44
John G.	1846	21- 90	John	1834	14-468
BURNEY, John	1796	5-364	CALVER, William	1787	4-190
BURNHAM, William	1830	13-391	CALVERT, Bathia	1733	2-286
BURNITT, Richard	1829	13-324	CAMERON, Hugh	1832	14-262
BURRALL, Charles	1836	16-141	CAMPBELL, Archibald	1805	7-396
BURRELL, Lindy	1803	7-173	Caleb	1838	17- 29
BURTON, Elijah	1834	15-162	Eleanor	1840	18- 8
Wm.	1770	3-138	Elizabeth	1818	10-431
BUSBY, John	1791	4-536	Francis, Jr.	1837	16-284
BUSH, James	1838	16-494	George	1794	5-152
John	1817	10-364	Isaac	1845	20-357
Joshua S.	1849	23-210	James	1778	3-463
Sarah	1818	10-476	James	1796	5-398
Shadrick	1826	12-280	John	1807	8-221
BUSK, James	1819	10-613	John	1822	11-379
BUSSEY, Edward	1787	4-245	Michael	1830	13-452
Jesse	1805	7-427	Moses	1815	10- 36
BUTLER, Amon	1806	8-152	Neal	1832	14-232
Amos	1804	7-320	Victor	1808	8-348
George	1817	10-324	William	1795	5-272
Henry	1746	1-367			

CANNE, Anthony	1836	16-122		Richard	1832	14-223
Felix	1806	8-109		Sarah	1834	14-432
CANNON, Isaac	1843	19-442	CARSIGNE, Louise L. A.	1805	7-388
Jacob	1843	19-436	CARSON, Joseph	1791	6-255
John	1781	3-420	CARTE, Hannah C.	1794	5-207
CANOLES, Charles	1841	18-396	CARTER, Bathia	1837	16-306
CANTWELL, Edward	1721	2- 6	Catherine	1849	23-232
Edward	1749	1-467	John	1797	5-499
CAPELL, Thomas	1703	1- 12	John	1814	9-477
CAPITO, Christina	1836	16- 23	Kitura	1822	11-489
George	1822	11-487	Richard D.	1841	18-193
CAPLES, Robert	1801	6-375	Robert	1804	7-264
CARBACK, Ephraim J.	1845	20-376	Sophia	1836	16- 69
		& 410	William	1782	3-467
CARE, Richard	1830	13-480	CARTWRIGHT, Abraham	1814	9-475
CAREY, Andrew	1786	4-169	Mary	1824	12- 59
James	1834	15-145	CARVER, Nathan	1845	21- 26
John	1839	17-195	CASEY, Eliza	1849	23- 83
Martha	1838	17- 11	Mary	1823	11-579
Richard	1844	20- 47	Robert	1796	5-413
CARLETON, Jane	1842	19-139	CASHION, Lawrence	1832	14-144
CARLIN, Aaron	1841	18-159	CASHLEY, James	1810	9- 1
CARLISLE, John	1747	1-407	CASSARD, Louis	1834	14-478
CARMACK, Joel R.	1850	23-456	CASTELLO, Francis	1845	20-411
CARNAN, Charles	1809	8-376	CATHERALL, William	1833	14-343
Christopher	1770	3-141	CATON, Mary	1846	21-295
Elizabeth	1830	13-477	CATTLE, John	1784	3-574
Robert N.	1836	16- 57	CATTS, John	1818	10-436
Sarah	1818	10-538	CAUSE, Bartholomew	1799	6-189
William	1842	19- 94	CAVE, Samuel J.	1847	22- 91
CARNIGHAM, James	1839	17-415	CAY, David	1797	5-514
CARNS, Samuel	1826	12-278	CAZEAH, Peter	1825	12-147
CAROTHREN, William	1739	1-311	CECIL, Ann	1819	10-565
CARPENTER, Uriah	1848	22-440	CHABERT, Anthony	1793	5-133
CARR, Elizabeth	1812	9-208	CHAFEE, Nathan	1835	15-368
Hetty	1834	15-174	CHAISTY, Ann	1849	23- 13
Thomas	1758	2- 78	Edward	1849	23-296
CARRERE, John	1841	18-409	CHALMERS, Prudence G.	1845	20-230
CARRINGTON, John	1696	1- 54	CHAMBERLAIN, John	1775	3-314
CARROLL, Aquila	1826	12-236	Margaret	1801	6-393
Charles	1783	3-503	Mary	1840	18-148
Charles, Jr.	1825	12-117	Matilda	1834	14-447
Charles	1834	1- 15	Samuel	1776	3-323
Daniel	1826	12-293	Samuel	1831	13-506
Henry H.	1804	7-331	CHAMBERS, Catherine	1832	14-117
James	1832	14-128	Daniel	1829	13-199
John	1815	10- 83	Elizabeth	1812	9-266
John	1830	13-489	Jane	1841	18-245
Marguerite	1817	10-294	Matthew	1825	12-155
Mark	1822	11-482	CHAMIER, Achsah	1785	4- 96

CHAMIER, Daniel	1779	3-595		CHRISTIE, Charles	1757	2-229
CHAMILLON, Joseph	1828	13-133		Gabriel	1808	8-312
CHAMPEL, Victor	1808	8-348		Robert	1780	3-392
CHANEY, Zephaniah	1823	11-599		CHRISTOPHER, James	1816	10-191
CHANDLER, Samuel V.	1847	22- 53		John	1834	16-159
CHAPLIN, David	1845	20-291		CHURCH, Amos	1807	8-247
CHAPMAN, Asall	1844	20-134		Elizabeth	1764	2-183
Elizabeth	1769	3-131		CHURCHMAN, Rebecca	1848	22-395
Hannah	1823	11-598		CITLER, Abraham	1800	6-243
Nathan	1807	8-198		CLAGETT, Alexander	1821	11-263
CHAPPELL, Thomas S.	1846	21-311		Eleanor	1830	13-383
CHARLES, Valentine	1807	8-321		Elie	1848	22-381
CHARNER, James	1837	16-296		Hezekiah	1834	14-412
CHASE, Charles	1839	17-300		Samuel	1825	12- 90
Elizabeth	1844	20-139		CLAIBORNE, Charles H.	1845	20-478
Hannah K.	1848	22-218		CLAP, Aaron	1834	15- 97
Peter	1838	22-301		CLAPHAM, George	1819	11 -65
Richard	1757	2- 76		Jonas	1841	18-222
Thomas	1779	3-378		CLARE, Alexander	1812	9-262
Thorndike	1838	17-106		CLAREY, Benjamin	1783	3-500
CHATFIELD, Elizabeth	1825	12-199		Nathaniel	1784	3-579
CHAYTON, James	1846	21- 71		CLARIDGE, Catherine	1846	21-210
CHAYTOR, Daniel	1830	13-430		CLARK, Dorcas	1829	13-262
CHENEY, Abel	1818	10-450		George	1813	9-289
George	1717	1-143		John	1827	12-415
CHENOWETH, Arthur	1802	6-533		Joseph	1799	6-229
Richard	1781	3-434		Neal	1776	3-326
Richard B.	1846	21-139		Rachel	1831	14- 39
Sarah	1848	22-346		Robert	1757	2-221
		& 406		Robert	1766	3- 50
Thomas	1846	21-245		Samuel	1798	6- 90
William	1820	11-158		Samuel	1832	14-185
CHESSON, John	1797	6- 29		Sophia	1798	6-127
CHESTON, Ann	1837	16-256		William	1825	12-215
CHEW, Anna Maria	1812	9-282		CLARKE, Eleanor	1850	23-479
Catharine	1848	22-277		James	1814	9-446
Henrietta	1848	22-477		James	1816	10-153
Joseph	1752	2- 42		John	1754	2- 48
William	1802	6-477		John C.	1841	18-232
CHILD, Henry	1832	14-179		Matthew	1818	10-416
CHILDS, George	1844	20-179		Richard	1813	9-315
Rebecca	1822	11-365		Robert E.	1802	7-164
CHIRAC, John F. C.	1832	14-161		Sarah	1802	7- 69
CHISHOLM, William	1821	11-262		Shammah	1849	23-286
TLER, Abraham	1800	6-243		William	1841	18-203
CHOATE, Edward	1841	18-161		William	1847	22-119
CHOCKE, John	1765	2- 13				& 250
CHOATE, Richard	1813	9-383		CLARKIN, Bernard	1832	14-254
Solomon	1791	4-545		CLARKSON, Thomas B.	1849	23-301
CHOCKE, John	1765	2- 13		CLAUR, William	1783	3-545

INDEX OF BALTIMORE COUNTY WILLS

CLAUTICE, Peter	1825	12-132		Charles	1823	11-571
CLAXTON, Alexander	1842	19- 59		Charles C.	1824	12- 77
CLAYTON, Richard	1821	11-258		Charles R.	1836	16-176
CLAYWELL, Maria D.	1846	21-253		Chloe	1824	11-640
CLEARY, Marie A.	1832	14-220		Edward	1795	5-229
CLEMENT, Leonard	1817	10-348		Edward A.	1834	15-107
CLEMENTS, Bede	1815	9-518		Eleanor	1795	5 -305
Joseph M.	1821	11-248		Elias B.	1838	16-463
CLEMM, Catherine	1836	15-467		Hiram	1841	18-382
CLEMONS, John	1783	3-519		John	1746	1-360
CLEMSON, Joseph	1830	13-415		John	1807	8-220
CLENDENEN, William H.	1840	17-448		John	1824	12- 70
CLENDENNING, Thomas	1762	2-149				79 &87
CLERY, Peter B.	1805	7-398		John, Sr.	1808	8-298
CLEVER, Barbara	1839	17-397		Joseph C.	1831	14- 31
CLOHERTY, Patrick	1806	8- 25		Joshua	1720	1-170
		& 26		Joshua	1765	3- 15
CLONET, Mary E.	1833	14-282		Joshua D. F.	1821	11-259
CLOSSEY, Johannah	1790	4-499		Joshua F.	1821	11-259
CLOSSEY, John	1785	4- 90		Lewis	1816	10-239
CLOUD, Cornelius	1843	21-407		Mary	1845	21- 15
COALE, Anne	1817	10-322		Melchor F.	1835	15-403
Cassandra	1746	1-368		Ruth	1816	10-179
Elizabeth	1828	13-102		Stephen	1797	5-529
George	1767	3- 58		Thomas	1785	4- 63
Hannah	1826	12-325		Thomas	1813	9-369
John	1746	1-373		Thomas	1824	11-651
John	1817	10-284		Thomas D.	1813	9-316
Joseph	1720	1-167		William	1756	2- 86
Philemon	1839	17-170		William	1775	3-317
Philip	1816	10-164		William	1846	21-196
Skipwith	1755	1-483		COCKSHAW, Aaron	1842	19- 80
William	1809	8-460		COFFIELD, James	1843	19-389
William	1817	10-276		COGGINS, John	1838	16-431
COAN, John	1748	1-421		Thomas	1821	11-216
COATES, Francis	1847	22- 22		COHEN, Maria I.	1834	14-477
Israel	1832	14-147		COLBERG, Christopher	1830	13-431
COBB, Daniel	1837	16-385		COLBERT, George	1819	11- 44
COCHET, Mary	1820	11-142		COLE, Abraham	1818	10-410
COCHRAN, Deborah	1821	11-276		Abraham	1822	11-404
Thomas	1807	8-209		Abraham, Sr.	1841	18-223
Thomas	1835	15-313		Abraham, of Wm.	1845	20-479
William	1818	10-438		Artridge	1850	23-372
William S.	1831	14- 14		Cornelius	1805	8- 6
COCKE, Dr. James	1813	9-358		Dennis G.	1773	3-252
COCKEY, Andrew R.	1821	11-275		Elizabeth	1812	9-210
Ann	1847	21-486		Frederick	1808	8-341
		& 496		George	1757	2-244
Caleb	1800	6-290		George	1762	2-134
Caleb	1829	13-177		George	1828	13-125

COLE, Henry	1840	18- 73
James	1772	3-211
John	1819	10- 60
Luther	1846	21-151
Mary	1815	9-253
Mordecai	1805	7-350
Rachel	1844	20-103
Richard	1805	7-410
Ruth	1843	19-233
Salathiel	1824	11-632
Samuel	1814	9-410
Samuel	1807	8-242
Sarah	1828	13-142
Thomas	1745	2-207
Thomas	1793	5- 53
Thomas	1810	9- 37
Thomas	1815	9-511
Vincent	1835	15-233
William	1758	2- 72
William	1770	3-144
William	1807	8-142
William	1822	11-456
COLEGATE, Benjamin	1762	2-127
John	1782	3-470
Richard	1721	1-498
Thomas	1795	5-249
COLER, John	1812	9-202
COLES, William	1842	19-135
Mary	1847	21-364
COLESWORTHY, John	1803	7-235
COLLADY, John	1805	8- 16
COLLETT, Daniel	1784	3-555
Mary	1849	23- 90
Moses, Sr.	1837	16-336
Nancy	1845	20-226
Ruth	1850	23-410
COLLINS, Daniel	1844	20- 56
James	1785	4-105
James	1841	18-348
James W.	1848	22-429
Joanna	1837	16-315
Patrick	1796	5-460
Peter	1810	8-492
William	1804	7-323
COLTRIDER, George	1833	14-386
COLVIN, Dr. Daniel	1803	7-172
John	1809	8-461
John	1818	10-471
Margaret	1806	8- 85
Margaret	1820	11-121
Samuel	1835	15-369

COLWELL, Thomas	1817	10-299
COMBEST, Jacob	1767	3- 67
COMEGYS, Benjamin	1809	8-418
John	1814	9-479
John G.	1819	10-572
Rachel	1841	18-269
COMPTON, John	1802	6-546
COMSTOCK, Job S.	1830	13-418
Matthew	1831	14- 92
CONKLIN, Anne	1838	17- 35
CONKLING, Eliza	1843	19-289
John A.	1849	23-233
		& 400
CONAWAY, Charles	1811	9-154
Solomon	1818	10-531
America	1823	11-614
CONN, Daniel	1794	5-159
Daniel	1836	16- 97
Elizabeth	1841	18-389
William	1821	11-311
CONNAWAY, John	1837	16-191
Perry	1846	21-137
CONNAY, Philip	1710	1- 34
CONNELLY, Bridget	1842	19- 60
CONNER, Hannibal	1813	9-317
James	1819	11- 18
John	1757	2-239
Margaret	1835	15-397
CONNOLLY, Henry	1830	13-458
CONRAD, Conrad	1769	3-102
CONSTANTINE, Richard	1833	14-286
CONWAY, John	1799	6-218
Robert	1801	6-384
CONYNGHAM, George	1825	12- 91
COOK, John	1768	3- 83
John	1804	7-266
Julianna	1832	14-221
alias Julianna Kime		
Thomas	1833	14-328
William	1829	13-164
William W.	1834	15-175
COOKE, Caleb	1842	19-170
Elizabeth	1836	16- 61
Francis	1843	19-235
Greenberry	1817	10-362
Henry	1810	8-503
Henry	1810	8-504
Robert	1822	11-356
Sophia	1838	16-494
William	1731	1-267
William	1739	1-322

COOKE, William	1817	10-338	COUREGES, James	1819	11- 11
COOKMAN, George G.	1841	18-406	COURSAULT, Edward	1814	9-480
COON, Margaret	1832	14-153	COURTNEY, Hercules	1816	10-210
COONEY, Patrick	1849	23-230	John S.	1827	12-340
COOPER, Bennett	1835	15-325	Mary	1818	10-598
Calvin	1819	11- 77	Mary	1826	12-263
Charles R.	1829	13-291	Robert	1807	8-207
Jane	1846	21-310	COVENHOVEN, William	1830	13-352
John	1759	2-296	COVENTRY, William	1699	1-177
John	1769	3- 33	COWARD, William	1805	7-434
John	1800	6-315	COWLEY, Elizabeth	1842	19- 22
John C.	1838	16-509	COWAN, John R.	1815	10- 66
Rebecca	1825	12-152	COX, Abriller	1847	21-421
Robert C.	1795	5-312	Amos	1849	23-416
Thomas	1805	7-343	Christopher	1713	1-105
COPELAND, John	1754	2- 52	Jacob	1798	6-121
William	1772	3-208	James	1777	3-338
COPEMAN, Peter	1807	8-223	James	1844	20-107
CORBETT, William	1797	6- 23	James, Jr.	1820	11-124
CORBEY, Elizabeth	1827	12-422	John	1830	13-459
CORBIN, Edward	1770	3-144	John	1831	14- 65
CORD, Thomas	1721	1-504	Kezia	1828	13- 57
CORNELIUS, Nicholas I.	1838	17- 46	Mary	1790	4-407
Peter	1849	23-158'	Peter	1837	16-325
CORNER, James J.	1843	19-424	COXE, Tench	1836	16- 31
CORNTHWAIT, Grace	1839	17-356	CRABTREE, William	1756	2-112
John	1782	3-446	CRADOCK, Arthur	1821	10-317
Robert	1800	6-322	Thomas	1770	3-147
		& 332	Thomas	1821	11·321
CORCORAN, Thomas	1828	13- 91	CRAFT, John B.	1829	13-275
CORRIE, James	1805	7-400	CRAGHEAD, Jemima	1787	4-249
CORSE, Israel	1850	23-440	CRAIG, Andrew	1843	19-272
COSFORD, Thomas	1675	1-102	Ann	1843	19-386
COSGROVE, Thomas	1831	14- 59	George	1816	10-102
COSKERY, Bernard	1837	16-322	Henry	1823	11-563
Felix	1783	3-531	James	1823	11-533
Francis	1799	6-230	John	1808	8-257
COTRAL, John	1730	1-246	John	1827	12-391
COTTAIN, William	1720	1-164	John	1839	17-294
COTTERRELL, John	1766	3- 38	CRAMER, Peter	1781	3-424
COUCHAND, Daniel	1764	2-180	CRAMLETT, Thomas	1817	10-367
COUGHLIN, Jeremiah	1846	21-182	CRAMPBLET, Mary A.	1818	10-449
alias COCHRAN			CRANDALL, John	1842	19-140
COULBORNE, Charles	1807	8-158	CRANE, Joseph S.	1839	17-275
COULSON, William	1826	12-299	CRANGLE, Henry	1819	10-592
COULTAM, Francis	1781	3-439	CRANSWICK, Thomas S.	1825	12-168
COULTER, Andrew	1798	6- 96	CRAWFORD, Andrew	1832	14-246
Matthew	1760	2-262	James	1756	2-107
COUNCELMAN, George	1794	5-196	Dr. John	1813	9-330
COUNCILMAN, George	1799	6-218	John	1797	8-538
George	1839	17-407	CREA, Hugh	1815	10- 15

INDEX OF BALTIMORE COUNTY WILLS

CREAMER, Henry	1803	7-129		Johanna	1756	2- 97
CREERY, John	1847	22-403		Richard	1785	4- 35
CREIGHTON, William	1757	2-227				& 38
CRESAP, Thomas	1790	4-398		Thomas	1802	7-110
CREVEY, Hans	1820	11-188		CRUSE, Jacob	1799	6-185
CROCKER, John	1817	10-326		CRYDER, Jacob	1776	3-328
Thomas	1792	5- 65		CUJAS, Francis	1793	5-138
CROCKETT, Gilbert	1772	3-233		CULBERT, Alice	1824	12- 14
John	1747	2- 12		CULLEN, Thomas	1731	1-256
CROMWELL, Benjamin	1828	13- 43		CULLIDON, George	1815	9-511
Comfort	1787	4-241		CULLISON, Shadrack	1821	11-328
Elizabeth	1800	6-244		William	1809	8-397
Jacob	1820	11-206		William	1818	10-435
John	1832	14-239		William	1824	12- 56
John G.	1801	6-439		CULVERWELL, Richard	1828	13-122
Joseph	1769	3-101				& 124
Joseph	1782	3-453		CUMMING, Hugh S.	1846	21-193
Mary	1817	10-229		CUMMINGS, Alexander	1774	3-294
O'Neil	1834	15- 41		James	1801	6-359
Nathan	1813	9-310		Jane	1841	18-293
Phebe	1816	10-141		Robert	1777	3-350
Richard	1717	1-144		CUMMINS, Margaret	1799	6-238
Stephen	1783	3-596		Robert	1794	5-151
Thomas	1723	1-223		CUNNINGHAM, John	1819	11- 22
Thomas	1817	10-317		John	1848	22-201
Urath	1838	17- 49		Matthew	1810	8-498
William	1684	1- 72		Michael	1786	4-125
CROOK, Charles	1826	12-322		William	1807	8-235
CROOKE, James	1727	1-236		CURL, William	1844	20- 61
Sarah	1737	1-288		CURRIER, Thomas	1780	3-400
CROOKS, John	1836	16-113		CURRY, Bartholomew	1843	19-277
CROSS, Barbara	1838	17- 19		John	1833	14-359
John	1763	2-179		CURRYER, William	1794	5-200
John	1846	21-229		CURTAIN, James	1802	7- 90
Nichodemus	1817	10-312		Jane	1847	22- 33
Rachel	1843	19-282		Thomas	1841	18-385
Solomon	1777	3-351		CURTIS, Abraham M.	1833	14-356
William	1770	3-148		Benjamin	1798	6-149
CROSSGROVE, Levi W.	1819	10-607		Jane	1834	15-177
CROTTINGER, Margaret	1816	10-178		CURTZ, Christopher	1794	5-163
CROW, James B.	1812	9-209		CUSHING, Margaret	1848	22-338
Rachel	1808	8-284		CUSHMAN, Thomas	1807	8-207
Sarah	1830	13-438		CUSTIS, Edmund	1808	8-317
CROWE, Isaac	1829	13-326		Elizabeth	1815	10- 87
CROWLEY, Dennis	1709	1- 36		CUTTER, Joseph	1809	8-383
CROW FIELD, Frederick	1848	22-294		CUZZINS, George	1816	10-123
CROXALL, Charles	1782	3-451				
Eleanor	1805	7-371				
		& 375		DAFAY, Michael R.	1796	5-361
James	1748	1-429		DAFFIN, George	1780	3-398
James	1809	8-426		DAGER, John	1798	6-133

DAILEY, John	1810	8-501	James	1815	10- 29
DAILY, Timothy	1843	19-475	James	1819	10-594
DALL, Eleanor	1829	13-294	John	1798	6-142
James	1809	8-354	John	1814	9-498
DALLAM, William	1834	14-493	Joseph	1798	6-124
DALLAS, William W.	1825	12-194	Joseph	1837	16-339
DALN, George	1823	11-590	Laurence B.	1834	14-447
DALRYMPLE, Frances	1826	12-238	Mary	1821	11-323
James	1824	12- 16	Mary H.	1840	18- 92
John	1817	10-365	Robert	1829	13-280
William	1813	9-355	Sarah	1796	5-362
DAMISH, Frederick	1827	12-414	Thomas	1748	1-432
DANE, John D.	1797	6- 66	Thomas	1784	4- 29
DANIELL, Charles	1737	1-289	Thomas	1834	15- 89
DANIELS, Anthony	1803	7-163	Uriah	1768	3- 97
DARBY, Daniel	1794	5-284	William	1807	8-258
Luke	1743	1-334	William	1808	8-338
DARE, Nathaniel	1815	10- 68	William	1840	18- 14
		& 111	Zachariah	1829	13-191
Sarah T.	1843	19-349	DAWES, Edward M.	1818	10-537
DARNAL, Henry B.	1793	5-121	James	1815	10- 7
DARNEL, Sampson	1819	11- 33	Molly	1839	17-390
DARING, Waltera	1837	16-259	DAWKINS, James	1764	2-171
DART, Joseph	1824	12- 16	DAWSON, James	1833	14-316
DASH, Denis	1830	13-434	John	1828	13- 49
DASHIELL, Henry	1830	13-481	William	1820	11-195
William A.	1780	5-395	DAY, Edward	1746	1-357
DASTE, John B.	1819	11- 5	Edward	1779	3-379
DAUGHADAY, John	1803	7-255	Edward	1842	19-142
DAUGHADY, Catherine	1826	12-299	John Y.	1805	8- 2
William H.	1824	12- 40	Laban	1750	2- 36
DAUGHERTY, William	1768	3- 85	Nicholas	1704	1- 74
DAVENPORT, Margaret	1845	20-490	Nicholas	1739	1-315
DAVEY, Alexander W.	1803	7-158	Rebecca Y.	1813	9-345
Elizabeth	1782	3-460	Sarah	1730	1-279
George	1795	5-290	DEADY, Daniel	1803	7-242
Samuel C.	1779	3-364	DEAL, Christian	1812	9-283
DAVIDGE, John B.	1829	13-268	Hannah	1844	20-45
DAVIDSON, Andrew	1787	4-239	John	1840	17-467
James	1806	8-102	Philip	1785	4- 83
James	1840	17-451	DEALE, Christian	1769	3-105
Job	1807	8-192	DEAN, Christian	1786	4-176
John	1797	6- 26	Hannah	1800	6-323
Martha	1797	6- 42	DEANS, Hugh	1777	3-326
Mary	1800	6-310	DEARING, John	1673	1-195
Robert	1820	11-202	DEAVER, Antill	1770	3-177
DAVIS, Anna	1803	7-167	Benjamin	1739	1-323
Archibald	1827	12-396	Emanuel K.	1844	20-122
Evan	1822	11-464	John	1731	1-270
Francis	1778	3-370	John	1782	3-476
Henry	1770	3-149	John	1813	9-352

DEAVER, Mary	1749	1-461
Philip	1785	4- 61
Rebecca	1793	5- 93
Richard	1745	1-410
Sarah	1766	3- 47
DE BAUFRE, James	1837	16-406
DEBRULAR, Mary	1751	3-415
William	1772	3-225
DEBRULER, George	1734	2-203
DECKER, Frederick	1804	7-328
Jacob	1827	12-434
John	1828	13-126
Lydia	1847	21-318
DECOURT, Maria H.	1818	10-499
Mark R. M.	1818	10-409
DEEDS, Michael	1789	4-388
DEEMS, Cornelius	1833	14-376
DEETS, John	1848	22-248
DEGAN, Henry U.	1827	12-416
also DEAGAN		
DEIL, Sophia	1840	17-446
DE LA TORRE, Jose J.	1827	1- 13
DELADEBAT, Augustus L. P.		
	1822	11-396
DELANCY, Maurice	1808	8-352
DELANY, Elizabeth	1807	8-155
DELASTRE, Michael F. A.		
	1797	6- 14
DELCHER, George	1817	10-337
Harriett	1825	12-173
John	1789	4-327
		& 329
John	1804	7-276
DELINOTTS, Eulalie	1832	14-219
DELOZIER, Ann	1835	15-315
Daniel	1813	9-365
DELUCA, Francis	1803	7-146
DEMMITT, John	1802	6-503
Richard	1766	3- 6
Thomas (Demitt)	1827	12-383
William	1751	3-419
William (Demitt)	1825	12-156
DEMONDIDIER, Anthony	1693	1-70
Anthony	1713	1-103
DEMPSTER, Ellen	1835	15-277
Thomas	1822	11-410
William T.	1836	16-123
DENEGE, Elizabeth	1694	1- 76
DENISON, Mary R.	1833	14-323
DENMEAD, Adam	1823	11-520

DENMEAD, John	1830	13-466
DENNIS, John	1792	5- 57
DENNY, Benjamin	1771	3-197
Michael	1819	10-607
William	1850	23-358
DENOS, Augustine	1806	8- 27
Mary	1811	9-161
DENT, Charles	1847	21-401
DENTLER, Margaret	1773	3-241
DENTON, John	1796	5-385
Margaret	1800	6-282
William	1747	1-414
DENYS, Benjamin	1818	10-402
DERSAA, Jean	1798	6-220
DERMANGIN, Charles	1817	10-264
DEROCHBRUNE, Lewis	1802	6-552
DESHON, Mary	1842	19-124
DESRAMEAUX, Appoline M. F.		
	1803	7-221
DESPEAUX, Frances A.	1835	15-426
otherwise Ann F. Despeaux		
DETMAR, Frederick	1818	10-435
DEVER, Elijah	1801	6-407
DEW, Anna	1826	12-295
James C.	1822	11-486
Rachel	1829	13-168
Robert	1808	8-308
Thomas	1758	2- 81
Thomas	1794	5-221
		& 227
DEWITT, Thomas	1807	8-222
DEYE, Penelope	1784	3-562
Thomas C.	1807	8-182
DICK, Ann	1817	10-303
George F.	1820	11-126
Thomas	1764	2-169
DICKERSON, Brittingham	1808	8-341
Daniel R. B.	1841	18-405
Lettis	1850	23-393
DICKEY, John	1792	5- 63
DICKS, Richard	1782	3-455
DICKSON, James	1769	3-118
John	1832	14-213
Priscilla	1835	15-334
William	1833	14-344
DIDIER, Henry	1822	11-459
Maria	1836	16-104
DIESELHORST, Charles	1845	20 -485
DIETER, Jacob	1793	5-125
DIETERLY, Christopher	1848	22-284

DIFFENDERFER, Dorothy	1829	13-325	DORROW, Daniel	1823	11-535
Elizabeth	1832	14-184	DORSEY, Benjamin	1829	13-270
John	1835	15-326	Comfort	1747	1-406
DIFFENDERFFER, Daniel	1819	10-598	Cornelius	1829	13-162
DIKEHUT, George	1817	10-268	Edward	1705	1- 47
DILLANEY, Isaac	1818	10-527	Edward	1782	3-483
DILLEHUNT, John	1832	14-171	Edward	1809	8-436
DILLING, James	1808	8-365	Edward, of Ed.	1839	17-266
DILLON, Henry	1771	3-198	Eleanor	1813	9-291
DILWORTH, Keziah	1848	22-214	Eleanor	1840	17-490
William	1807	8-145	Elias	1794	5-193
DIMMITT, Rose	1831	14- 64	Elizabeth	1815	9-527
William	1846	21-183	Elizabeth	1840	18- 84
DIMOND, William	1824	12- 32	Elizabeth, of C.	1844	20- 99
DINENBERGER, George	1844	20-157	Ezekiel J.	1827	12-350
DINSMORE, Henry W.	1814	9-474	Francis	1749	1-455
DISNEY, James	1843	19-343	Francis	1769	3-128
Solomon	1808	8-317	Harriet	1849	23-303
DISTANCE, Hetty	1836	15-453	Jane P.	1843	19-302
DITTMAR, Christopher	1799	6-226	John	1714	1-128
DIVERS, Christopher	1766	3- 33	John E.	1841	18-375
Christopher	1828	13-132	Josiah	1819	10-551
DIXON, Thomas	1849	23-102	Lydia	1807	8-258
DOBBIN, George	1811	9-199	Margaret	1829	13-170
Hugh	1799	6-203	Maria	1826	12-290
Thomas	1808	8-292	Nancy	1841	18-392
DOBLER, John M.	1838	16-490	Nicholas	1717	1-142
DODD, George	1842	18-479	Nicholas	1780	3-344
John	1801	6-473	Owen	1825	12-121
DODDS, Margaret	1807	8-219	see also pages 132, 173, 174		
DODGE, Samuel	1803	7-208	Samuel	1724	1-211
DOLLY, Henry	1797	6- 65	Samuel	1818	10-414
DONAHUE, Henry	1722	1-196	Thomas I.	1838	17- 6
Roger	1748	1-438	William	1847	22-128
DONALD, William	1827	12-332	DOSH, Rebecca	1847	21-292
DONALDSON, Frances	1837	16-364	DOSSIOUS, George	1797	6- 37
James	1803	7-229	DOSSON, John J.	1845	20-316
Thomas	1800	6-245	DOUGHERTY, Elizabeth	1846	21-181
William	1835	15-239	Elizabeth	1849	23-109
DONCER, Peter F.	1800	6-343	James	1836	16-177
DONNELL, John	1827	12-424	John	1828	13- 80
Mary A.	1836	15-473			& 215
DONNELLAN, Thomas	1810	9- 57	John	1830	13-350
DONNELLY, Patrick	1827	12-406	Theophilus F.	1822	11-474
Peter	1825	12-136	DOUGLASS, Benjamin	1828	13-154
DONNOLLY, William	1843	19-250	Richard N.	1829	13-297
DONOVAN, Valentine	1835	15-425			& 460
DOP, George	1813	9-312	Sarah	1833	14-291
DORLING, Monies	1794	5-190	DOWDLE, George	1815	10- 36
DORMAN, Mary	1843	19-372	DOWIG, George	1807	8-161

DOWLING, Edward	1845	20-377	Thomas	1816	10-154
William	1835	15-238	DUKE, Charles	1801	6-349
DOWNES, John	1718	1-315	Christopher	1749	1-457
DOWNEY, Thomas	1809	8-450	Christopher	1788	4-290
DOWNS, Jesse	1849	23-142	Christopher	1799	6-157
DOWSON, Joseph	1816	10-183	DUKEHART, Henry	1807	8-249
DOYLE, Mary	1792	5- 38	John	1842	19-185
Mary	1848	22-486	Margaret	1824	12-209
Patrick	1838	17-160	Parthenia	1843	19-478
Richard	1791	5- 31	Sarah G.	1848	22-175
Sarah	1796	5-369	DUKES, Henry	1717	1-146
Thomas	1809	8-424	DULANEY, Thomas	1749	1-318
DRAKE, Ann H.	1832	14-247	DULANY, Ann	1829	13-203
Martha L.	1820	11=118	Daniel	1797	5-499
DRAPER, Lawrence	1713	1-123	Daniel	1825	12-209
DRAUBAUGH, John	1810	9- 25	Rebecca	1823	11-585
DREEVIS, Harman	1794	5-145	DUMAS, Mary	1849	22-491
DRESHER, Henry	1808	8-340	DUMOUSSAY, Francis	1794	5-352
DREW, Anthony	1720	1-154	DU MOULIN, James	1821	11-279
Bennet	1813	9-309	DUNAH, Adolphus	1838	16-512
George	1735	1-277	DUNBAR, George T.	1843	19-241
Margaret	1721	1-514	DUNCAN, Annie T.	1848	22-182
DRIGGS, Asa	1829	13-319	DUNLOP, William	1772	3-232
DRISDALL, Robert	1784	4- 88	DUNN, Dennis	1748	1-442
DROHAN, Thomas	1826	12-239	James	1807	8-260
DRURY, William	1837	16-239	John	1761	2-353
DRYDEN, Milby	1812	9-207	Robert	1769	3-130
DRYSDAL, Thomas	1798	6- 84	William	1825	12-158
DUBEMAT, John A.	1844	20-203	DUNNING, George	1850	23-414
DUBERNARD, William	1841	18-452	DUNNOCK, Catherine	1836	16- 19
DUBLIN, Thomas	1813	9-359	John, Sr.	1819	11- 50
DU BOISMARTIN, Francis A.			Joseph	1836	16- 16
	1833	14-351	DUNWOODY, Robert	1824	12- 37
DUCATEL, Adme	1833	14-388	DUPOUSE, Anthony	1798	3-375
DUCHEMIN, Francis A. C.	1818	10-466	DURBIN, Christopher	1709	1- 25
Margaret	1841	18-163	John	1743	1-343
DUCHENET, Peter D.	1798	6-107	DURDIN, James	1848	22-208
DUCKETT, Ann	1808	8-290	DURDING, John T.	1842	19-168
Thomas, Jr.	1807	8-151	Joseph	1805	7-412
DICKHART, Volerius	1783	3-527	DURHAM, John	1695	1- 51
DUDLEY, John L.	1842	19-133	Samuel	1703	1-176
DUESBURY, Elizabeth	1836	16- 72	Samuel	1772	3-218
*DUFF, William	1848	22-288*	DURKEE, Pearl	1826	12-225
DUFFANT, John B.	1811	9-159	Robert A.	1848	22-329
DUFFY, James	1828	13- 93	DU ROBERIT, Francis M. I.	1799	6-198
Mary K.	1818	10-414	DURST, John F.	1838	16-461
*DUFAY, Charles	1795	5-270*	DUSSERRIL, Jacques	1801	6-465
DUGAN, Cumberland	1834	16-130	DUTTON, Robert	1770	3-150
Hammond	1841	18-378	DUVALL, Ann S.	1846	21-146
Mary	1816	10-209	Richard	1846	21-252

DWYER, Jane	1815	10- 5		ELIVES, William	1815	9-513
Patrick	1809	8-413		ELLENDER, Frederick	1841	18-300
DYE (DEYE), Thomas C.	1807	8-182		ELLETT, George	1748	1-446
DYKEN, John	1797	5-539		ELLICK, Catherine	1827	13- 1
DYSART, Esther	1824	11-632		ELLICOTT, Andrew	1809	8-429
Mary	1843	19-291		Andrew	1823	11-519
				Esther	1830	13-455
				George	1832	14-167
EAGER, John	1722	1-185		James	1820	11-163
Thomas	1708	1- 8		John	1814	9-407
EAGER, Thomas W.	1825	12-167		John	1820	11-186
EAGLESTON, Abram	1823	11-553		John	1823	11-574
EAGLESTONE, Abraham	1783	3-494		John M.	1841	18-461
EARBY, Ann	1832	14-177		Jonathan	1825	12-175
EARP, Joshua	1812	9-267		Mary	1842	19-109
EASTER, Ira A.	1840	17-457		Mary A.	1843	19-279
Jane A.	1840	18- 26		Sarah	1840	17-458
EASTMAN, Henry	1821	11-235		ELLIOTT, Benjamin	1834	14-445
EATON, John	1789	4-341		Benjamin	1838	16-468
EAVERSON, Catherine	1832	14-218		George	1824	12- 78
Thomas	1814	9-473		Henry	1842	19-205
EBAUGH, Catherine	1803	7-227		James	1786	4-173
Henry, of George	1839	17-305		James	1809	8-409
John	1833	14-396		James	1816	10-139
EBSWORTH, George D.	1831	14- 60		Joseph B.	1826	12-315
EDDRIE, Charles	1821	11-297		Mary	1816	10-163
EDMONDSON, Isaac	1822	11-477		Mary	1832	14-145
Thomas	1837	16-211		Michael	1808	8-526
EDWARDS, Elizabeth	1846	21-288		Thomas	1807	8-245
James	1811	9-150		William	1781	3-424
John	1770	3-148		ELLIS, Daniel	1825	12-182
Thomas	1784	3-589		Reuben	1796	5-409
William	1777	3-340		Samuel	1847	21-354
EGAN, Andrew	1845	21- 1		ELLOT, James	1843	19-456
EGERTON, William	1836	15-468		ELLOTT, Shadrick	1811	9-176
EGLIS, William	1826	12-261		ELLRICK, Amelia	1812	9-277
EHLER, Ulrick	1762	2-129		ELVINS, Elizabeth	1838	17- 28
EHRMAN, John	1810	9- 28		ELWELL, Joshua	1844	20- 17
Margaret	1836	16- 79		ELWOOD, Thomas	1799	6-223
EICHELBERGER, Barbara	1819	10-498		ELY, William	1838	16-475
Jacob	1832	14-250		EMERSON, Benjamin	1848	22-339
Louis	1836	16-163		Sarah	1832	14-122
Mary E.	1832	14-242		EMMART, William	1842	19- 66
EISELEN, Frederick	1829	13-160		EMMERSON, Arthur	1828	13- 34
EISELL, John	1835	15-374		Mary	1826	13- 86
ELDER, Rebecca H.	1843	19-377		Patrick H.	1821	11-234
Ruth	1827	12-409		EMMERT, Henry	1844	20- 33
Sally	1840	18- 74		EMORY, John	1836	15-436
ELGARD, Elizabeth, alias Elgard				Robert	1848	22-275
Elliott	1824	12- 7		Thomas L.	1835	15-301

EMPSON, James	1707	1- 99		John	1827	12-339
EMRICK, Nicholas	1829	13-284		Job, Jr.	1775	3-312
ENGLAND, James	1830	13-390		Job	1780	3-400
ENLOES, Abraham	1709	1- 28		Margaret	1829	13-276
Anthony	1750	2- 33		Oliver	1821	11-241
Hendrick	1708	1- 17		Thomas	1828	13- 78
ENNALLS, Andrew S.	1803	7-210		William	1807	8-199
ENNIS, Gregory	1844	20-172		EVALT, Edward	1824	12- 13
Philip	1826	12-227		Ellenora	1833	14-355
ENSOR, Ann	1841	18-371		John	1839	17-439
Darby	1825	12- 96		EVANS - see above.		
Eleanor	1801	6-447		EVERET, John	1758	2- 84
Eleanor L.	1837	16-375		John	1760	2-271
Elizabeth	1815	10- 51		EVERETT, Thomas	1817	10-336
Geprge	1771	3-197		EVERHART, George	1835	13-317
George	1804	7-296		Paul	1761	2-356
George	1827	12-360		EVERIN, David	1756	2-117
Jemima	1810	8-480		EVERLY, Margaret	1814	9-425
Jemima	1837	16-279		EVERSON, Nicholas	1821	11-271
John	1773	3-257		EWELL, John	1835	15-374
John, Sr.	1831	14- 26		Sophia A.	1843	19-311
		& 28		EWING, Robert	1831	13-499
John, Sr.	1835	15-337		Thomas	1780	3-402
Martha	1822	11-366		EWINGS, John	1709	1- 23
Nathan	1843	19-449				
William	1834	15-132				
ENTLER, Salome	1849	22-488		FACE, Charles	1815	10- 96
ENTWISLE, John J.	1846	21-273		FAER, Edward	1805	7-352
ENTZ, Andrew	1841	18-335		FAGG, Amos	1762	2-136
EPAUGH, Jacob	1790	4-496		FAIR, George, Jr.	1818	10-524
ERDMAN, Peter	1833	14-330		FAIRBAIRN, Maria E.	1828	13- 48
ERHART, Nicholas	1845	20-289		FAKES, Harriet	1832	14-264
ERICKSON, Mary W.	1848	22-204		FALLOW, John	1806	8- 28
		255 &280		FARBER, Adam	1783	3-523
ERNST, Catherine	1819	11- 59		FARFAR, William	1721	1-516
ERRICKSON, Errick	1752	2- 41		FARMER, John	1845	20-246
ESENDER, Thomas	1818	10-400		FARRA, Mary	1815	10- 2
ESMENARD, Jean F.	1813	9-324		FARRELL, George	1827	12-336
ETCHBERGER, William	1823	11-538		James	1819	10-554
Wolfgang	1828	13- 77		Mary A.	1831	14- 59
ETINNE, Frederick	1794	5-277		FARRICA, Robert	1805	7-397
ETTING, Hetty	1847	22- 74		FASBENNER, Elizabeth	1828	13- 42
Kitty	1838	16-485		FAVERGER, Charles L. F.	1839	17-198
Solomon	1847	22- 46		FAVIER, Anthony	1833	14-348
EULER, Nicholas	1825	12-134		FEAR, Barton	1821	11-236
EVANS, Daniel	1812	9-250		FEARSON, Jesse	1838	16-444
David	1766	3- 53		FEATHER, Henry	1785	4- 55
Elizabeth	1818	10-535		FEINOUR, Charles	1849	23-202
Evan	1721	1-181		FELKS, Ann	1720	1-168
Jane	1813	9-356		FELL, Edward	1743	1-271

FELT, Edward	1766	3- 29	William	1825	12-165
Eley	1797	6- 63	FITE, Abigail	1839	17-444
Elijah	1810	9- 1	Jacob	1806	8- 47
Stephen	1790	4-482	FITZGERALD, James	1786	4-126
William	1786	4-175	John	1791	4-547
FELPS, Thomas	1748	2- 75	Richard	1806	8- 83
FENDALL, Edward	1835	15-227	FITZPATRICK, John	1850	23-364
FENN, Edward	1844	20- 55	FITZSIMMONS, Nicholas	1743	2- 10
FENNE, Joseph	1850	23-488	FLACK, James	1841	18-205
FENTON, James	1836	15-480	FLANAGAN, Charles	1766	3- 24
FENWICK, Thomas	1702	1- 53	Edward	1765	3- 28
FERGUSON, Benjamin	1828	13- 81	FLATT, Ann	1784	3-552
Mary	1835	15-386	FLAX, John	1809	8-418
Sarah	1824	12- 71	FLEMING, Mathias	1810	9- 41
FERNANDIS, John	1850	23-421	FLING, Joseph	1767	3- 66
FERBELL, John	1815	16- 79	FLINN, James	1806	8-363
FERRY, John	1698	1- 38	Patience	1824	12- 80
FETCH, Elizabeth	1793	5-108	FLINT, William	1838	16-511
FIELDS, John	1820	11-100	FLINTOFF, John	1820	11-113
FIFER, John	1831	14- 8	FLOYD, Andrew	1798	6-103
FIMESTOR, Alexander	1844	20- 92	Rev. John	1797	6- 23
FINAGAN, Henry	1765	3- 12	Joseph	1825	12-182
John P.	1810	8- 470	Thomas	1739	1-319
FINK, Adam	1832	14-142	Thomas	1822	11-365
FINN, Elizabeth	1841	18-450	FOARD, Benjamin	1844	20-103
FINSHAM, Elizabeth	1738	1-303	Jeremiah	1812	9-232
FISHBURN, Philip	1796	5-410	FOBLE, Elizabeth	1796	5-450
FISHER, Charles	1842	19-128	FOLKS, Thomas K.	1848	22-137
Daniel	1800	6-248	FOLTZ, Jacob	1821	11-221
Francis E. C.	1847	22-108	William	1810	8-482
George	1797	6- 6	William	1818	10-496
George	1845	21- 7	William F.	1837	16-361
George N.	1848	22-391	FONERDEN, Adam	1817	10-378
James A.	1827	12-359	FOOS, John	1821	11-296
Joseph	1833	14-380	Samuel	1848	22-245
Leonard	1801	6-371	William	1801	6-472
Michael	1799	6-174	William	1829	13-193
Michael	1799	6-182	FORD, George	1819	11- 78
Peter	1788	4-310	Jeremiah	1812	9-232
FISHPAW, John	1825	12- 84	John	1782	4-456
FISHWICK, James	1800	6-306	John H.	1810	9- 34
FISK, John	1819	10-579	Joseph	1790	4-431
FISSOUR, John M.	1816	10-234	**Joseph T.	1843	19-367
FITCH, Ai	1810	9- 5	Rebecca	1814	9-469
Douglas	1849	23-37	Rebecca	1837	16-367
John	1830	13-399	Samuel	1838	16-510
Pleasancey	1849	23- 51	**Lloyd	1818	10-494
Robert	1809	8-411	Thomas	1748	1-435
William	1788	4-284	Thomas	1842	19- 27
William	1804	7-321	FOREMAN, Leonard	1833	14-355

INDEX OF BALTIMORE COUNTY WILLS

FOREMAN, Leonard	1840	18- 86	FOXCRAFT, James	1839	17-225
FORGE, Marguerite	1792	5- 52	FOY, Frederick, Sr.	1839	17-302
FORMAN, Jane	1836	15-485	James	1816	10-102
FORNEY, Daniel	1846	21-283	Michael	1787	4-201
David	1827	12-357	Miles	1751	3-412
Elizabeth	1819	10-590	FRAISSE, Elizabeth I.	1820	11-116
Peter	1840	18- 9	FRANCE, Peter	1849	23-105
Matthias N.	1837	16-332	Thomas	1832	14-191
FORNSHIL, John	1848	22-174	FRANCIS, William	1770	3-146
FORSTER, Francis G.	1830	13-465	FRANCOISE, Marie	1830	13-433
George	1850	23-353	FRANK, Elizabeth	1811	9- 96
FORSYTH, Alexander	1829	13-329	Mary M.	1847	21-378
Alexander, Sr.	1829	13-211	Philip	1797	5-535
Rachel	1840	18- 38	FRANKLIN, Benjamin	1794	5-177
William	1828	13- 63	Joseph	1850	23-455
FORT, Alfred I.	1842	19-195	Thomas	1794	5-178
Elizabeth	1804	7-330	FRANKFORTER, Nicholas	1795	5-225
Joshua	1833	14-317'	FRASER, Elenor	1795	5-353
Samuel	1749	1-449	FRAZIER, Andrew	1826	12-246
FORTE, Benjamin	1843	19-283	Henrietta M.	1846	21- 86
FORTUNE, James	1797	6- 53	John	1756	2- 94
FOSS, George	1828	13- 16	John	1784	3-553
FOSSBENDER, Peter	1823	11-592	John	1785	4- 85
FOSTER, Aaron	1803	7-223	Joshua	1799	6-171
Isabella	1830	13-464	Penelope	1848	22-450
John	1826	12-232	Solomon	1826	12-242
FOSTREE, Edward	1744	1-395	FREE, John	1814	9-424
FOULK, Louis	1835	15-388	FREELAND, Catharine	1826	12-306
FOULKS, Joseph	1737	1-292	John	1802	7- 20
FOUNTAIN, Collier	1781	3-420	John	1825	12-101
FOUSE, Henry	1816	10-195	Stephen	1708	1- 24
Theobald	1828	13-101	Uriah	1849	23-280
FOWBLE, Catherine	1803	7-144	FRENCH, Benjamin	1804	7-272
Melchor	1838	17- 75	James	1760	2-281
Sabina	1841	18-199	John	1774	3-289
FOWLDS, Thomas	1806	8- 39	John	1839	17-433
FOWLE, John	1787	4-199	Samuel	1808	8-311
FOWLER, David	1841	18-191	Samuel A.	1810	9- 72
John P.	1850	23-356	FRESH, Francis	1814	9-396
Mary	1846	21-122	FREUND, Jacob	1847	22- 88
Richard	1817	10-355	FREY, Henry	1834	15- 50
Richard	1836	16- 51	FREYER, Henry	1835	15-376
Samuel	1812	9-227	FRICK, Ann B.	1836	16- 1
Sarah	1840	17-454	Jacob	1835	15-356
Thomas	1786	4-180	Peter	1827	12-411
FOWLEY, Michael	1841	18-220	FRIESE, John F.	1830	13-491
FOWNES, John	1802	7-72	FRIEZE, Simon	1835	15-330
FOX, John	1849	23-110	FRINGER, Margaret	1844	20-143
FOXALL, Elizabeth	1813	9-333	Michael	1814	9=485
Thomas	1812	9-247	FRISBIE, William	1837	16-234

FRISBY, Eleanor	1030	16-350	GARDNER, George	1833	14-404
FRITZ, Joseph	1828	13-120	George	1846	21-269
FROLIC, Charistian	1783	3-522	John	1741	1-376
FROST, Francis	1848	22-472	John	1799	6-162
FRY, William	1768	3- 82	Martha W.	1822	11-493
FRYE, Joseph	1845	20-362	Mary	1849	23- 96
FUDGE, William H.	1813	9-244	Robert	1711	1- 80
FUGATE, Martin	1837	16-289	William	1824	12- 7
FULFORD, Eleanor	1815	10- 81	GAREY, Jeremiah	1828	13- 20
Henry	1841	16-318	GARLAND, Nathaniel	1847	21-480
William	1838	16-501	GARNER, Thomas, Jr.	1850	23-459
FULLER, John	1843	19-456	Willis B.	1839	17-253
Nicholas	1808	8-351	GARRET, Elizabeth	1831	14- 92
Samuel	1808	8-339	Isaac	1773	3-243
FUNCK, Bendict	1834	14-443	GARRETSON, Garrett	1804	7-282
FUNDERLAND, Michael	1827	12-394	Isaac	1830	13-463
FUSSELBAUGH, John	1814	9-400	GARRETTSON, James	1764	2-368
			Job	1806	8- 89
			John	1773	3-279
GAFFORD, Joseph	1824	12- 41	Martha	1767	3- 62
GAHNER, Henry	1848	22-444	Mary	1835	15-294
GAINE, William	1693	1- 79	Shadrick	1787	4-266
GALBRAITH, Barbara	1832	14-261	Sophia	1769	3-110
John	1785	4- 46	Thomas H.	1849	23-223
William	1788	4-112	GARRISON, Benjamin	1820	11-189
GALE, Elizabeth	1714	1-125	Mary	1822	11-424
GALLAGHER, Alexander	1816	10-145	GARTS, Charles	1811	9-162
Eleanor	1835	15-423	GARTY, Frederick	1795	5-288
Elizabeth	1832	14-157	GASH, Nicholas	1769	3-103
Jane	1844	20- 9	Thomas	1704	1- 81
Patrick	1849	23- 98	Thomas	1759	2-308
GALLEGA, Francis	1848	22-295	GASSAWAY, John	1769	3- 94
GAMBLE, Nicholas	1813	9-386	GATCH, Benjamin	1816	10-250
GALLION, John	1731	1-253	Conduce	1797	6- 47
GALLOWAY, Mary	1838	17-112	Elizabeth	1847	21-336
Moses	1798	6-122	Godfrey	1759	2-302
Pamela	1803	7-137	Mary	1816	10-130
Robert C.	1844	20- 1	GATCHELL, Elizabeth	1830	13-377
Sarah	1826	12-264	Jacob	1823	11-530
William	1785	4-100	GATES, Joseph	1772	3-224
William	1705	1- 49	GAY, Ann	1786	4-166
William	1743	1-348	Nicholas R.	1770	3-151
William	1811	9- 98	GEARY, James	1832	14-191
GALLUP, Rufus B.	1847	22- 65	GEDDES, Elizabeth	1821	11-320
GAMBLE, Nicholas	1813	9-386	Sarah	1839	17-232
GAMBRELL, John	1843	19-314	GEER, Thomas	1809	8-442
GANDIN, Joseph	1788	4-289	GEILL, Richard	1846	21-211
GANTEAUM, James	1829	13-273	GEISLER, George D.	1839	17-425
GAST, Anne	1818	10-537	GELBACH, Christian	1847	22- 55
Peter	1831	14-106	Sarah	1848	22-320
GARDINER, Christopher	1725	1-208	GEORGE, Archibald	1840	18- 52

INDEX OF BALTIMORE COUNTY WILLS

GEORGE, Guild	1801	6-455	GILLES, David	1824	12- 10
William E.	1839	17-238	Henry N.	1834	15-211
GEPHARD, John F.	1812	9=242	Marie P.	1849	23-214
GEPHART, Frederick A.	1830	13-430	Robert	1807	8-252
GERMAN, Jonathan	1847	21-409	William R.	1820	11-205
Mary C.	1812	9-204	GILESPIE, William	1797	6- 9
Philip	1814	9-476	GILLESPY, Edward	1829	13-198
GETTIER, Peter K.	1849	23- 88	GILLET, Martin	1837	16-382
GETTINGER, Conrad	1823	11-614	GILLIAT, Susan H.	1847	21-356
GHEQUIERE, Charles	1818	10-505	GILLINGHAM, George	1827	12-328
GIBBS, John	1835	15-366	John	1806	8- 46
Nicholas	1814	9-490	John	1848	22-316
GIBSON, Francis	1766	3- 37	Mary	1850	23-354
Gabriel	1845	20-308	GILLORD, Thomas	1708	1- 96
James	1830	13-334	GILMOR, Elizabeth W.	1848	22-198
Joseph	1849	23- 95	John	1849	23-201
Robert	1704	1- 83	Louisa	1827	12-430
Thomas B.	1801	6-417	Robert	1822	11-360
William	1832	14-174	Robert	1848	22-451
William L.	1849	23-278	William	1829	13-275
GIFFORD, John	1818	10-477	GINHART, F. H.	1828	13-114
Mary	1847	22-106	GINSBACK, Jacob	1809	8-447
GILBERT, Cook	1820	11-174	GIRAUD, John J.	1839	17-257
Eleazer	1843	19-305	GISSE, Susanna	1815	10- 55
Jarvis	1739	1-305	GIST, Cornelius H.	1830	13-482
Thomas	1714	1-124	Elizabeth	1826	12-247
GILBRAITH, Margaret	1806	8-113	George	1820	11-170
GILCRESH, Robert	1767	3- 65	George R.	1845	20-388
GILCREST, Hellen	1772	3-220	John	1782	3-466
GILDEN, John B.	1845	20-277	Mordecai	1792	5- 59
GILDES, Felix	1836	16-115	Penelope D.	1820	11-175
GILES, Cassandra	1755	2- 54	Rachel	1826	12-246
John	1725	1-203	Rachel	1831	13-504
John	1736	1-280	Susannah	1803	7-152
Nathaniel	1730	1-243	Thomas	1788	4-297
Rebecca	1814	9-482	Thomas	1813	9-384
GILL, Edward	1818	10-539			458&522
Edward	1835	15-335	GITTINGER, Elizabeth	1831	14-102
John	1797	5-467	Jacob	1843	19-317
John	1822	11-472	John	1793	5- 9
John, Jr.	1839	17-194	GITTINGS, Archibald	1832	14-162
Leah	1843	19-284	Elizabeth	1831	14- 42
Nicholas	1796	5-348	James, Jr.	1820	11-128
Prudence	1833	14-296	James	1823	11-523
Sarah	1822	11-479	Mary	1847	22- 95
Stephen, Jr.	1717	1-150	Mary	1825	12-174
Stephen	1735	2-202	Mary	1841	18-263
Urith	1800	6-325	Peggy	1824	12- 53
GILLARD, Jacob	1824	12- 72	Rebecca M.	1844	20- 71
GILLES, Clara A.	1836	15-460	Sarah	1849	23- 36

GITTINGS, Thomas	1760	2-259		Samuel	1843	19-238
Thomas	1784	4- 1		William L.	1834	15- 62
GIVIN, John	1815	10- 99	CORE, Charles	1808	16-420
GLADMAN, Michael	1789	4-381		Christian	1802	7-126
Michael	1818	10-497		George	1814	9-390
GLASS, William	1848	22-394		Hannah	1827	12-381
GLAZIER, John	1830	13-397		Jacob	1790	4-505
GLENN, Elias	1846	21- 46		John	1808	8-353
Samuel	1802	7- 15		Michael	1793	5- 96
John W.	1828	13- 74		Nicholas	1813	9-303
GLINN, Thomas	1795	5-296		Philip	1818	10-503
GLOVER, John	1803	7-251	GORMACON, Michael	1725	1-214
Margaret	1810	9- 31	GORMELY, Owen	1800	6-284
GODDARD, Ann	1846	21-161	GORNLEY, James	1839	17-205
Mary K.	1816	10-213	GORSAGE, William	1797	5-534
GODFROID, William	1818	10-451	GORSUCH, Agnes	1848	22-405
GODSGRACE, William	1782	3-480		Charles	1792	5- 69
GOETZ, Francis S.	1844	19-502		Charles	1806	8- 58
John	1817	10-269		Charles	1816	10-126
Rachel	1848	22-433		David	1784	4- 3
GOGINS, Thomas	1821	11-216		David	1841	18-398
GOHLINGHORST, Mary A.	1847	22- 23		Hellen	1823	11-522
GOLD, Harriot	1848	22-403		Henry	1819	11- 66
Oliver	1787	4-227		John	1796	5-371
Paul	1839	17-379		John, of John	1843	19-316
Peter	1848	22-342		John M.	1845	20-419
GOLDER, Sarah	1836	16-181		Joshua	1797	6- 5
GOLDING, Arabella	1811	9-196		Joshua	1844	20-145
GOLDSMITH, Elizabeth	1837	16-309		Loveless	1783	3-492
George	1692	1- 73		Mary	1805	8- 18
John	1846	21-222		Mary	1821	11-265
Thomas	1800	6-279		Nathan	1788	4-317
GOLDTHWAIT, Mary	1821	11-301		Nicholas	1839	17-341
See also Gouldthwait.				Pellasha	1834	14-465
GOODHAND, Robert	1831	14- 66		Richard	1834	14-470
GOODING, Thomas	1849	23- 43		Robert	1720	1-166
GOODMAN, John	1799	6-209		Sarah	1802	6-536
GOODWIN, Ann	1837	16-402		Thomas	1774	3-315
Ann	1840	18-130		Thomas	1777	3-333
Eliza	1834	15- 54		William	1846	21-107
Joshua	1822	11-384	GOSNELL, Charles	1831	14- 54
Dr. Lyde	1801	6-432		Greenbury	1848	22-369
Milcah	1829	13-244		James	1837	16-416
Pleasance	1777	3-354		Peter	1787	4-228
Susannah	1834	15-209		Warnall	1778	3-309
William	1809	8-447		William	1762	2-143
GOOTEE, Elizabeth	1844	20-110		Zebediah	1807	8-217'
GORDON, Charles	1784	4- 12	GOSS, Dennis	1805	7-413
George	1806	8-507	GOSTWICK, Aquilla	1781	3-422
Ross	1800	6-240		Joseph	1728	1-217

GOTT, Edward	1823	11-508		Daniel	1817	10-289
Rachel	1797	6- 2		Eleanor	1813	9-350
Richard	1751	3-417		Elizabeth	1836	16- 41
Richard	1793	5- 87		Jane	1831	14- 34
Richard	1843	19-245		Jane	1846	21-189
Robert	1832	14-255		Jeremiah	1813	9-342
Ruth	1842	19- 25		John	1826	12-227
Samuel	1787	4-225		John	1830	13-337
GOTTSCHER, Henry	1847	22- 73		Mary	1848	22-333
GOUGH, Benjamin	1810	9- 31		Rebecca	1850	23-324
Harry D.	1808	8-315		GRAVENSTINE, Dorothy	1838	17-130
Prudence	1822	11-439		GRAVES, Alice	1818	10-522
GOULD, James	1809	8-430		Ebenezer	1823	11-588
John	1823	11-583		Robert	1847	21-404
Mary T.	1841	18-473		Thomas	1784	3-563
GOULDSMITH, Johanna	1687	1- 40		GRAY, Ann	1756	2-116
GOULDTHWAIT, Samuel	1806	8-100		George	1828	13-148
Winkles B.	1806	8- 93		James	1824	12- 60
See also Goldthwait.				John	1832	14-161
GOURDON, Ferdinand	1834	15-199		John	1844	20-131
Sarah	1849	23- 85		Lynch	1826	12-305
GOUVENOUR, Isaac	1825	12-160		Mary	1822	11-387
Nicholas	1835	15-360		Patrick	1755	1-493
GIVAN, William	1768	3- 78		Rebecca	1844	20-118
GOVANE, James	1784	3-570		Samuel	1793	5-116
William J.	1807	8-256		Zachariah	1747	1-403
GOVER, Elizabeth	1764	2-186		Zachariah	1778	3-371
Ephraim	1770	3-154		GRAYBELL, Philip	1821	11-312
Samuel	1744	2- 23		Philip	1831	14-100
GOWAN, John	1834	15- 29		GREAT, Jacob	1838	16-460
GRACE, James H.	1847	21-477		GREEN, Abednego	1839	17-327
John	1818	10-413		Abraham	1832	14-268
Peter B.	1835	15-399		Benjamin	1819	10-603
Philip	1777	3-343		Benjamin	1826	12-237
GRAFF, Mary E.	1847	22- 62		Bennett	1800	6-331
GRAFTON, William	1759	3-125		Charles	1831	14- 82
William	1767	3- 56		Clement	1796	6-486
GRAHAM, Daniel	1771	3-186		Elizabeth	1820	11-106
Irvine	1837	16-233		Hannah	1798	6- 80
James	1795	5-307		Henry	1820	11-153
John	1778	3-367		Henry	1833	14-341
Mary	1849	23-197		Henry	1839	17-328
GRAINGER, William	1802	7- 66		Hugh	1784	4- 6
GRAMBERY, John	1847	21-342		Isaac	1800	6-277
GRAMES, Hugh	1801	6-358		Isaac	1828	13- 64
GRAMMER, Eliza	1849	23-240		Jesse	1834	15-163
GRASMUCK, Casper	1770	3-155		John	1848	22-147
GRANGETT, Andrew	1785	4- 57		Joseph	1813	9-302
GRANT, Alexander	1738	1-297		Josias	1841	18-350
Charles	1836	16- 56		Josias M.	1835	15-371

GREEN, Lydia	1817	10-387		John	1781	3-563
Moses	1795	5-268		John	1792	5- 32
Nathan	1814	9-488		John	1794	5-188
Nathaniel E.	1850	23-413		Matthew	1822	11-352
Peter	1815	10- 71		Nathan	1806	8-104
Rebecca	1836	16-182		Robert	1848	22-152
Robert	1774	3-296		Sally	1788	4-319
Samuel	1823	11-618		Samuel	1745	2-210
Sarah	1827	12-346		Sarah	1842	19-152
Shadrach	1822	11-483		Thomas W.	1838	17- 4
Solomon	1806	8-103		William H.	1836	16-173
Vincent	1800	6-333		York	1796	5-401
Vincent	1850	23-326		GRIFFITHS, Richard	1842	19- 50
William H.	1839	17-343		GRIMES, Anna C.	1821	11-275
GREENALL, Robert	1756	1-494		Catherine	1834	14-498
GREENFIELD, Elizabeth	1831	14- 62		Nicholas	1768	4-308
James	1779	3-385		William	1830	13-477
John	1832	14-154		GRINDALL, Christopher	1749	1-451
Micajah	1773	3-255		GROC, Ann	1843	19-225
Nathan	1826	12-258		GROGG, Jacob	1807	8-186
Thomas	1705	1-141		GROOM, William	1826	12-249
William	1763	3- 4		GROOMRINE, George	1779	4-110
GREENWOOD, Francis P. W.	1845	20-382		GROOMS, Nathan	1836	16- 42
GREER, James	1742	1-340		GROSS, Christian	1845	20-248
GREGG, Alexander	1850	23-365				& 362
GREGORY, Ann	1837	16-218		John	1840	18- 16
Caty	1799	6-155		GROSSCUP, Frederick	1849	23-213
John	1826	12-304		GROVE(R)MAN, Anthony	1847	22-107
Simon	1736	1-273				$ 132
GRENAN, Richard	1819	11- 49		GROVE, Stephen	1818	10- 53
GRENIFF, John	1708	1- 26		GROVER, George	1729	2-193
GRESHAM, Margaret	1826	12-286		George	1786	4-110
GRICE, Edward	1844	20-197		GROVES, Dorothy	1720	1-165
		& 292		GRUNDY, John	1778	3-368
George	1825	12-140		GRUPY, Francis	1849	23-241
Sarah	1836	15-466		GUEST, Sally H.	1845	20-304
GRIEST, Isaac	1802	7-123		GUFFIN, Andrew	1799	6-187
Mary	1814	9-499		GUICHARD, John P.	1807	8-138
GRIFFEE, Richard	1812	9-237		GUILFOIL, Richard	1833	17-163
GRIFFIN, Benjamin	1843	19-292		GUITON, Henry	1816	10-128
John	1844	20-116		Underwood	1824	12- 52
Joseph	1827	13- 5		GUN, John	1799	6-166
Susanna	1815	10- 33		GUNBY, Ann	1812	9-271
GRIFFITH, Abraham	1800	6-268		GUNN, Bernard	1839	17-237
Ann	1835	15-324		GUNTER, Stephen	1808	8-367
Benjamin	1799	6-181		GUNTRUM, Christian	1845	21- 8
Catherine	1828	13- 21		GUTHROT, Joseph	1811	9-129
Eliza A.	1848	22-475		GUTHROW, John	1831	14- 63
Jacob	1837	16-295		GUTTORY, James	1819	10-604
James	1778	3-366		GUY, David	1727	1-238

GUYTON, Benjamin	1766	3-339	Tilley	1812	9-215
Benjamin	1801	6-419	HALL, Ann	1799	6-196
John	1843	19-426	Ann	1830	13-411
Sarah	1832	14-214	Aquilla	1815	10- 9
GWEEN, George	1795	5-332	Avarilla	1755	1-492
GWINN, Charles	1837	16-221	Catherine	1836	15-465
GWYNN, Achsah	1833	14-278	Charlotte	1848	22-232
Eleanor	1829	13-271	Daniel	1842	19- 32
John	1833	11-553	Don C.	1823	11-603
Mary	1801	6-460	Edith	1834	15-340
William	1819	11- 82	Elisha	1772	3-220
			Elisha	1814	9-443
			Elisha I.	1833	14-324
HACK, Andrew	1845	21- 3	Elizabeth	1840	18-136
HACKERMAN, Henry H.	1815	10- 46	Edward	1742	1-332
Susanna	1812	9-254	Edward	1763	2-365
HACKETT, Jane	1850	23-325	Edward	1800	6-329
Joseph P.	1845	21- 23	Edward	1843	19-294
Margaret	1828	13- 56	Edward	1848	22-190
Susan F.	1846	21-134	Elisha. See above		
Lydia	1840	18-154	Elizabeth. See above.		
HADDON, William	1762	2-157	Harriott I.	1806	8- 37
HADEN, William	1802	7- 12	Henrietta	1828	13- 38
HADLEY, John	1807	8-224	Henry	1725	1-206
HADSKIS, Samuel H.	1825	12-149	Isaac	1777	3-336
Sarah	1830	13-428	Jacob	1842	19-197
HAETTINGER, Michael	1830	13-366	Jonathan	1735	1-283
HAGEDOM, John A.	1802	7-111	John	1718	1-133
HAGER, John	1841	18-366	John	1737	1-285
HAGERTY, John	1824	11-635	John	1768	3- 89
Sarah	1839	17-167	John	1847	21-426
HAGTHROP, Edward	1843	19-224	John, Jr.	1770	3-158
HAHN, John	1850	23-403	John M.	1842	19- 88
HAIG, Margaret	1846	21-226	Joshua	1782	3-481
HAILE, Charles	1845	20-305	Josias C.	1814	9-494
Jane	1820	11-126	Levin	1829	13-248
Neal	1796	5-402	Levin	1842	19-104
Sarah	1796	5-404	Margaret	1803	7-228
HAINES, Catherine	1801	6-346	Mary	1774	3-291
Michael	1818	10-452	Mary	1841	18-342
HAINS, George	1829	13-208	Mary	1845	20-279
HAIR, Jacob	1828	13- 33	Mary L.	1844	20- 69
Tamer	1833	14-318	Nicholas	1730	1-248
Strophel	1812	9-242	Osborn S.	1845	21- 2
HALBERT, Ann	1849	23-252	Richard W.	1847	22- 83
Edward	1849	23-10	Robert L.	1847	21-405
HALDEMAN, Henry	1849	23-117	Susan F.	1847	22- 77
HALDER, Mary	1819	11- 41	Susanna	1823	11-549
HALE, Neal	1813	9-368	William	1815	9-552
Thomas	1821	11-249	William	1836	16- 75

HALLACK, Elizabeth	1803	7-134		Andrew	1812	9-224
HALLTINGER, Michael	1830	13-360		Elizabeth	1841	18-379
HAMILTON, Edward	1830	13-447		Grizelda	1815	10- 92
Edward S.	1849	23-129	HANNAH, Robert	1839	17-263
Hugh	1845	20-415	HANNAN, John	1820	11-183
John A.	1838	17- 34	HANNER, John	1823	11-534
Robert	1829	13-186	HANNON, Patrick	1784	4- 28
Samuel	1839	17-209	HANSELL, Benjamin	1812	9-222
Sarah	1788	4-304	HANSON, Edward	1785	4-107
Thomas	1805	7-451	Halbert	1778	3-363
Thomas	1824	11-628	Hollis	1747	1-411
William	1759	2-315	Jacob	1766	3- 16
William	1770	3-160	Jonathan	1786	4-115
William	1801	6-427	Joseph	1812	9-223
HAMM, Thomas	1800	6-247	Mary	1778	3-373
HAMMELL, James	1787	4-271	Mary	1794	5-197
HAMMER, Ann	1825	12-213	Rebecca D.	1837	16-347
Peter	1816	10-173	Ruth	1831	14- 7
HAMMOND, Ann	1784	4- 14	Sarah	1742	1-335
Beale	1797	6- 61	Thomas	1714	1-115
Harnet	1826	22-262	HARCHMAN, Thomas	1734	2-203
John	1739	1-307	HARDEN, Frances	1816	10-255
John	1805	7-392	Susan	1846	21-186
John	1780	3-393	William	1848	22-423
Joseph	1843	19-229	HARDESTY, Ann	1821	11-270
Margaret	1822	11-477	HARDESTER, Benjamin	1842	19-187
Mathias	1798	6-139	HARDING, Ann	1842	19-172
Mordecai	1797	6- 1	Hiram	1839	17-399
Nathan	1818	10-398	Ignatius	1808	8-345
Rebecca	1805	7-394	James	1775	3-311
Rezin	1783	3-549	HARDISTY, Henry	1848	22-182
Rezin	1796	5-432	HARDY, George	1805	7-406
Thomas	1724	1-209	Robert W.	1843	19-403
Thomas	1761	2-332	William	1830	13-358
William	1752	2- 36	HARE, Elizabeth	1815	10- 86
William	1785	4- 40	Jacob	1824	11-625
William	1785	4- 82	Michael	1850	23-371
HAMPSHIRE, Elizabeth	1841	18-169	Philip	1836	15-449
HAMSHIRE, George	1827	12-400	HARENT, Joseph	1818	10-477
HANCE, Mary	1825	12-273	HARGEST, James	1843	19-260
HANCOCK, Robert	1837	16-236	HARGOOD, Margaret	1819	10-599
HANDLEN, Patrick	1823	11-522	HARGROVE, John	1839	17-428
HANDLIN, Mary	1850	23-369	Thomas	1804	7-327
HANDS, Ephraim	1831	14- 93	HARKER, John	1842	19-137
HANEWALT, Ludwick	1818	10-500	HARLAN, Samuel	1850	23-401
HANEY, Michael	1784	4- 21	HARLEY, John	1787	4-206
HANLAN, William	1844	19=500	HARMAN, John	1812	8-211
HANLEY, Peter	1842	19- 84	Sarah	1799	6-177
HANN, John	1848	22-365	HARTNETT, James	1805	7-386
HANNA, Alexander	1765	3- 22	HAROD, Susannah	1765	3- 13

HARPER, Charles C.	1837	16-387		Margaret	1813	9-338
Mary	1822	11-359		Rachel	1817	10-301
HARRIMAN, John	1710	1- 29		Samuel D.	1846	21- 50
See also Harryman.				William	1774	3-288
HARRINGTON, Thomas	1842	19-167		HARWOOD, Asenath	1830	13-335
HARRION, Joseph	1817	10-388		James	1847	21-495
HARRIS, Carey A.	1843	19-244		James	1848	22-291
David	1809	8-458		Lucy	1836	16- 25
Edward	1724	1-212		Sarah	1833	15-341
Edward	1773	3-237		Thomas	1827	12-344
Edward	1828	13- 70		HASENCLEAVER, Casper	1810	8-487
John F.	1834	15-186		HASFELDT, John	1828	11-429
Mary Ann	1769	3-126		HASKINS, Joseph	1806	8-127
Prince	1800	6-267		William	1789	4-349
Robert	1839	17-371		HASLETT, Ann	1814	9-483
Thomas	1740	1-323		William W.	1814	9-482
Thomas	1748	1-440		HASLEWOOD, Henry	1699	1-178
William	1777	3-341		HASLUP, Jesse	1838	16-531
HARRISON, Hall	1830	14-457		HASSANER, George	1848	22-382
Jonathan	1831	14- 48		HASTINGS, John	1724	1-213
Susan	1834	15- 96		HATHAWAY, John	1839	17-417
Thomas	1782	3-474		HATTON, Aquila	1816	10-184
Thomas	1808	8-279		Chaney	1803	7-233
William	1815	10-100		John	1770	3-159
William	1841	18-156		John	1815	10- 11
William	1848	22-241		Unity	1774	3-296
HARRYMAN, David	1845	20-397		HAUBERT, Elizabeth C.		
George	1774	3-285			1846	21-280
George	1794	5-236		Frederick	1818	10-460
John	1748	1-431		HAUCK, Barnet	1835	15-350
John	1784	4- 16		HAUGHEY, Sarah	1835	16- 54
Joshua	1799	6-239		HAUPTMAN, John	1827	12-432
Thomas	1733	2-283		HAWKER, John P.	1830	13-456
William	1812	9-285		HAWKINGS, Samuel	1849	23- 16
See also Harriman.				HAWKINS, George	1835	15-242
HART, Charles	1805	8- 11		John	1733	2-287
Dorothy	1817	10-344		John	1811	9-141
John	1799	6-236		Joseph	1725	1-222
Joseph	1815	10- 74		Matthew	1705	1-138
Lewis	1848	22-259		Matthew	1762	2-146
Mary	1813	9-367		Robert	1761	2-344
William	1823	11-513		Thomas	1715	1-116
HARTLEY, Samuel	1830	13-401		William	1711	1- 94
HARTMAN, Christopher	1799	6-158		William	1818	10-480
HARTSINK, Peter	1808	8-322		HAWLEY, Ann	1827	12-393
HARTWAY, Ann E.	1786	4-141		HAWS, Dearing	1763	3- 78
Vitus	1777	3-345		HAY, Elizabeth K.	1840	18-115
HARVEY, Abarilla	1822	11-395		George	1813	9-326
Elizabeth	1824	11-635		Robert	1806	8-126
Margaret	1789	4-389		HAYDEN, Agnes A.	1836	15-481

HAYDEN, James	1825	12- 88
Michael	1830	13-416
William	1802	7- 12
William	1817	10-296
HAYDOCK, John	1807	8-214
HAYES, Frances	1804	7-306
John	1822	11-464
Joseph	1807	8-233
William	1842	19-117
HAYLEY, Valentine	1808	8-343
HAYS, Francis	1778	3-356
John	1726	1-235
HAYWARD, Harriet	1815	10- 35
Joseph	1777	3-345
Thomas	1811	9- 93
William	1814	9-416
HAYWORTH, Jonathan	1830	13-465
HAZLETT, Robert	1824	12- 38
HEADINGTON, Michael	1801	6-388
William	1782	3-487
HEALEY, John	1848	22-322
HEARN, Sarah	1843	19-307
HEARTLE, Isaac T.	1836	16- 11
HEATH, Hannah	1833	14-358
James	1766	3- 32
Thomas	1698	1-136
HEATHCOTE, John	1814	9-438
HEBB, John	1839	17-233
HEDDINGER, Barbara	1804	7-290
HEDDINGTON, Elizabeth	1810	9- 63
HEENEY, Cornelius	1849	23-177
HEFFERNAN, William	1810	9- 9
HEIDE, George	1829	13-309
HEINZMAN, Samuel	1801	6-383
HEIR, Philip	1772	3-226
HELEMS, Daniel	1846	21-276
HELITAS, Mary M.	1805	7-424
HELM, Elizabeth	1847	21-335
James	1812	9-240
Leonard	1794	5-139
Mary	1792	5- 56
Mary	1793	5- 81
Mary, alias Sparrow	1811	9-123
Mayberry	1790	4-487
HELMS, Ann	1776	3-324
Anna M. G.	1832	14-150
HELPHENSTONE, Lydia H.	1815	10- 55
HEMMEL, Anna Maria	1809	8-384
HEMPHILL, Andrew	1837	16-344
HENDERSON, Andrew	1848	22-145

HENDERSON, Archibald	1813	9-351
Robert	1790	4-484
HEADLEY, Paris	1817	10-374
HENDON, Josias	1738	1-303
Hannah	1748	1-442
Joseph	1760	2-280
Josias	1738	1-303
Richard	1768	3- 86
HENDRICKSON, John	1781	3-442
HENDRIX, Adam	1837	16-186
HENESTOFILL, Barnet	1822	11-381
HENIS, Frederick	1829	13-189
HENNICK, Barbara	1827	12-354
HENNING, Thomas	1830	13-454
HENRY, Benjamin	1825	12-166
Elizabeth	1815	10- 52
John	1770	3-157
John	1841	18-387
Mary	1773	3-239
HENSON, David	1845	21- 10
Edney	1849	23-158
HERBERT, Frances	1844	20-188
John	1808	8-311
HERINS, Solomon	1830	13-406
HERMANGE, Anthony	1811	9-146
Francis P.	1833	14-391
Peter	1845	20-410
HERN, Araminta	1845	20-386
HEROLD, George D. C.	1811	9-173
HERRING, George A.	1846	21-298
HERRON, James	1841	18-167
HERSHEY, Barbara	1845	21- 11
HESLIP, John	1830	11-190
HESS, Joseph	1842	18-497
HESSELIUS, Mary	1820	11-147
HESSONTON, William	1802	7- 7
HEVENER, Eliza	1849	23-304
Samuel	1838	16-484
HEWES, Jones	1839	17-337
Joseph V.	1848	22-150
HEWITT, Caleb	1805	7-356
Richard	1729	1-244
Robert	1827	12-337
HEYDE, Anthony	1843	19-327
HEYLAND, Marcus	1813	9-387
HEYRIG, John	1816	10-236
HICKEY, Amelia	1805	7-442
Cornelius	1783	3-533
William	1805	7-399
HICKLEY, Robert	1845	21- 24

HICKLEY, Sarah	1799	6-216		HIPWELL, Sarah	1834	14-405
Sebastian	1827	12-348		HISS, Elizabeth	1842	19- 56
William	1833	14-328		Jacob, Sr.	1839	17-363
HICKS, Abraham	1822	11-368		HISSEY, Charles	1812	9-240
Ann	1783	3-495		Henry	1781	3-441
Charles G.	1845	20-451		Henry	1841	18-291
George	1842	19- 59		William	1849	23- 53
Henry	1751	3-415		HITCHCOCK, George	1747	1-400
Jacob	1816	10-243		Robert	1831	14- 90
Nehemiah	1769	3-115		William	1738	1-294
William	1710	1- 44		HITCHEW, Philip	1772	3-228
HIGDIN, Benjamin D.	1841	18-265		HOBBY, Sarah	1814	9-428
HIGGINBOTHOM, Thomas	1842	19-265		HOBERT, John B.	1785	4- 95
HIGGINS, Janet	1849	23-256		HOBSON, George	1830	13-486
HIGGINSON, Nancy M.	1849	23- 80		HOCHSTATTER, John D.	1802	7-124
HIGHAM, John	1850	23-427		HOCHSTETTER, Margarette		
HIGSON, George	1829	13-279			1833	14-290
HILBERT, Barbara	1829	13-328		HODGE, John	1790	4-409
John A.	1841	18-303		Margaret	1794	5-156
Sophia	1831	13-501		HODGES, John N.	1845	20-395
HILL, James M.	1849	23- 26		William	1812	9-218
John	1692	1- 52		HODGKIN, Thomas B.	1805	7-415
John	1768	3- 92		HOFFMAN, Andrew	1825	12- 99
John	1827	12-398		Anna M.	1848	22-437
Joseph	1763	2-178		Daniel	1842	19-157
Moses	1763	2-363		Frederick G.	1815	10- 66
Rodger	1675	1- 49		George	1834	15- 72
William	1682	1- 60		Jeremiah	1844	20-163
William	1703	1- 92		Jeremiah T.	1849	23-313
William	1765	3- 24				& 496
HILIARD, Benjamin F.	1841	18-393		John	1837	16-271
HILLEN, John	1727	1-239		Peter	1837	16-261
John	1840	18- 71		William	1811	9-144
Solomon	1801	6-379		William	1829	13-167
Solomon	1841	18-331		William A.	1842	19- 7
Thomas	1848	22-154		HOFNER, John L.	1827	12-342
HILTON, John	1784	4- 21		HOGARTH, George	1822	11-499
Martha	1835	15-385		HOLLAN, Mary F.	1846	21-282
HICKS, Mary	1798	6- 89		HOLLAND, Daniel	1849	23-311
HINDES, James B.	1847	21-490		Francis	1746	1-374
HINDMAN, James	1830	13-369		Francis U.	1819	10- 46
HINDMARCH, Mary	1814	9-414		John	1793	5-118
HINES, Elizabeth	1756	2-103		John F.	1732	1-261
Thomas	1755	1-487		Thomas	1818	10=473
HINKLE, William	1829	13-257		William	1727	1-240
HINSON, Joseph	1821	11-228		HOLBERT, George	1847	21-494
Joseph	1849	23-209		HOLLBROOK, Jacob	1809	8-464
HINTON, Milcah	1818	10-457		HOLLER, Francis	1783	3-524
Samuel	1720	1-159		Philip	1795	5-264
HIPPS, Lewis	1828	13- 22		HOLLETT, Cornelius	1846	21-307

HOLLIDAY, Daniel C.	1834	15- 83	
John R.	1800	6-270	
Robert	1747	1-399	
William	1824	12- 12	
HOLLINGSWORTH, Ann	1824	12- 73	
Elizabeth	1840	18- 61	
Francis	1826	12-235	
George	1703	1- 77	
George	1755	1-490	
Jesse	1810	9- 42	
Levi	1822	11-451	
Rachel L.	1819	10-581	
Samuel	1830	13-411	
HOLLINS, Cordelia M.	1848	22-169	
William	1810	9- 81	
William	1845	20-466	
HOLLIS, Peter	1828	13- 90	
William	1680	1-174	
William	1763	3- 2	
HOLMES, Ann	1847	22-105	
Delilah	1816	10-116	
Gabriel	1819	10-585	
James	1805	7-366	
Jonathan	1833	14-374	
John	1813	9-344	
John	1822	11-495	
Mary	1815	10- 75	
Mary	1832	14-163	
Oliver	1839	17-404	
Richard	1836	16-176	
Thomas	1841	18-377	
HOLT, Henry E.	1845	20-489	
John	1758	2- 83	
HOLTER, Anthony	1814	9-478	
Theresa	1814	9-477	
HOLTZ, John P.	1821	11-300	
HOLTZINGER, Barnet	1772	3-214	
Jane	1826	12-251	
HOMES, Gabriel	1819	10-584	
HONEY, Amos	1833	14-277	
HOOD, Sarah S.	1849	23-310	
HOOK, Anthony	1800	6-409	
Ferdinand	1826	12-282	
Jacob	1801	6-344	
Jacob	1815	10- 50	
Jacob	1841	18-310	
Joseph	1773	3-246	
Joseph, Sr.	1838	17-156	
Rudolph	1775	3-209	
Rudolph	1823	11-616	
Ursula	1804	7-325	

HOOKER, Aquilla	1791	5-10	
Jacob	1816	10-251	
John	1806	8- 40	
Richard	1781	3-428	
Richard	1846	21- 93	
Samuel	1773	3-239	
Susanna	1830	13-427	
Thomas	1744	2- 16	
Thomas	1817	10-304	
HOOPER, Abraham	1804	7-325	
Jacob	1837	16-298	
James	1837	16-378	
James	1846	21-198	
Joseph	1739	1- 84 & 317	
William	1836	16- 14	
HOOPS, Adam	1771	3-259	
HOOS, John	1799	6-180	
HOPE, George	1721	2- 1	
HOPEWELL, Henrietta R.	1845	20-339	
HOPKINS, Brian	1848	22-340	
David	1824	12- 4	
Ezekiel	1815	9-526	
Gerrard	1800	6-260	
Gerard T.	1834	14-496	
Hopkins	1809	8-423	
John	1785	4- 45	
John	1818	10-430	
John	1850	23-391	
Johns	1837	16-372	
Joseph	1808	8-328	
Mary	1820	11-196	
Richard	1785	4- 49	
Richard P.	1842	19- 29	
Robert	1703	1- 13	
Samuel	1767	3- 59	
Sarah	1793	5-112	
William	1823	11-547	
HOPKINSON, Mary	1836	16-180	
HOPPE, Justus	1846	21-241	
HORN, Christopher	1799	6-158	
George	1836	15-439	
Henry M.	1822	11-428	
Martin	1799	6-233	
William	1705	1- 44	
HORNBY, Gualter	1816	10-270	
HORNER, Francis	1817	10-300	
Thomas	1756	2- 98	
HORNES, Joseph	1820	11-127	
HORSEY, Lazarus	1816	10-201	

HOSE, Catherine	1831	14- 31	HOY, John	1804	7-262
HOSGOOD, William	1830	13-474	HUBBELL, Josiah	1838	17-150
HOSHEL, Mary	1845	20-442	Samuel	1836	16-118
HOSSEFARTZ, George	1801	6-386	HUBER, Henry	1827	12-380
HOSSELBACK, George	1850	23-489	HUBERT, Joseph	1801	6-426
HOUCHINS, William	1749	1-470	HUDSON, Jonathan	1786	4-179
HOUCK, Jacob	1835	15-428	Robert	1813	9-324
HOUGH, Robert	1810	8-469	Robert W.	1833	14-333
HOUGHTON, Henry A.	1840	18- 50	HUGG, Benjamin	1809	8-453
HOUK, Jacob	1828	13-128	Jacob	1800	6-283
HOULDMAN, Abraham	1668	1- 61	HUGHES, Ann	1830	13-490
HOULTON, Mary	1847	21-442	Barnabas	1765	3- 11
HOURSTON, Elizabeth	1847	22-132	Charles	1788	4-301
John	1804	7-279	Charles I.	1839	17-441
HOUSE, Ephraim	1838	17-145	Christopher	1849	23-228
HOUSTON, John	1844	20-223	Emmeline	1825	12- 88'
HOW, Edward	1779	3-378	Francis	1840	18-121
HOWARD, Charles	1799	6-161	George A.	1850	23-470
Cornelius	17777	3-355	Hannah	1770	3-158
Cornelius	1844	20- 10	Hannah	1816	10-143
Dinah	1836	16-124	James	1819	10-576
Edmond	1745	2-215	James	1824	12- 9
Eve	1813	9-314	James	1847	21-413
Francis H.	1814	9-468	Jane	1765	3- 27
Henry	1817	10-342	John	1791	4-526
Johanna	1763	3- 7	Laura S.	1833	14-383
John	1826	12-234	Peter	1847	21-337
John B.	1835	15-430	Samuel	1771	3-185
John E., Jr.	1822	11-501	Sarah	1810	9- 4
John E.	1827	12-408	William	1815	10- 51
Joshua	1738	1-296	HUGHS, Mary	1828	13-141
Lemuel	1759	2-306	William	1748	1-436
Margaret	1844	20-177	HULSE, Matthew	1797	6- 34
Mary	1829	13-174	HUMPHREY, Hugh	1829	13-220
Mary W.	1844	20-219	William	1845	21- 18
Mary W.	1847	21-389	HUMOHREYS, Parker	1817	10-366
Prudence	1847	22- 1	Thomas	1734	2-204
Ruth	1796	5-442	HUMOHRIES, Catharine	1786	4-114
Thomas	1838	16-481	HUMSTEAD, Elizabeth	1690	1-137
William	1717	1-147	HUNN, Christian W.	1845	21- 28
William	1834	15-105	HUNT, Enoch	1850	23-340
William G.	1848	23-442	Job	1809	8-381
HOWE, Martha	1836	16-184	John H.	1826	12-277
HOWELL, Ann E.	1832	14-173	Phinehas	1837	16-215
William	1824	12- 34	Samue 1 C.	1839	17-330
HOWEY, Susannah	1813	9-332	Susanna	1847	21-351
HOWKE, Barenhard	1782	3-478	Thomas	1842	19- 4
HOWLAND, Daniel	1837	16-248	HUNTER, George	1797	6- 4
HOWLET, Mary	1794	5-211	Henry	1837	18-319
HOWLETT, John	1819	11- 32	James	1784	4-41
HOWSER, John	1829	13-330			

HUNTER, John	1834	15-188
Peter G.	1838	17-147
Rebecca	1836	16-174
Robin A.	1840	17-489
HURD, John	1778	3-360
HURST, William	1830	13-485
HUSBAND, William	1773	3-275
HUSMAN, John F.	1841	18-307
HUSSEY, Asahel, of George		
	1839	17-284
George	1819	10-580
Nathan	1814	9-408
Hutchins, Ellen N.	1838	16-526
James	1818	10-528
Jemima	1839	17-389
Joseph	1841	18-276
Joshua	1819	11- 88
Mary R.	1841	18-280
Nancy	1833	14-347
Nicholas	1794	5-210
Nicholas	1808	8-350
Nicholas	1843	20-355
Sarah	1845	20-402
Thomas	1732	1-264
Thomas	1817	10-282
Thomas	1848	22-417
William	1824	12- 55
		& 124
William, Jr.	1827	13- 11
HUTCHINSON, James	1825	12-175
John	1840	18- 79
Phebe	1796	5-429
HUTSON, George	1846	21-267
Martha	1848	22-325
HUTTON, Elijah	1849	23-128
James	1838	16-453
Samuel	1816	10-259
William	1789	4-385
HUYGHE, Ann	1840	18-102
John J.	1824	12- 67
IGOW, Lewis	1760	2-281
ILGER, George	1793	5- 91
INGLIS, James	1826	12-230
Mary	1830	13-426
INGRAM, John	1733	2-294
John	1740	1-329
Ruth	1782	3-445
INIS, Alexander	1821	11-273

INLOES, Abraham	1790	4-510
INNIS, John	1817	10-291
IRELAND, Edward	1816	10-202
Elizabeth	1844	20- 39
IRVINE, Alexander	1821	11-238
Ann	1819	10-585
Mary H.	1837	16-290
IRWIN, Constant	1769	3-127
ISAACKE, Elizabeth	1824	11-623
ISAACS, William C.	1837	16-225
ISRAEL, Anne	1836	16-155
Beal	1830	13-434
Fielder	1848	22-389
Gilbert	1788	4-299
Gilbert	1834	15-185
ISRAELL, John	1723	1-202
JACKSON, Abraham	1787	4-275
Bolton	1838	16-516
Frances	1843	19-220
Gilbert	1817	10-327
Henry	1704	1-139
Henry	1817	10-334
Isaac	1748	1-439
James	1698	1- 58
James	1718	1-126
John	1848	22-321
Joseph	1821	11-264
Matthew	1813	9-227
Patience	1763	2-364
Rachel	1832	14-255
Samuel	1720	1-163
Thomas	1704	1- 95
Thomas	1821	11-216
Thomas	1842	19-170
William	1816	10-218
William	1820	11-198
William	1847	21-360
JACOB, George	1846	21-119
Jane	1837	16-300
Samuel	1839	17-372
William	1804	7-298
JACOBS, Elias	1841	18-204
Solomon	1830	13-362
JACQUETT, Rebecca	1846	21-204
JAFFRAY, Alexander	1822	11-335
James	1820	11-131
JAGER, Jasper	1808	8-332
JALLAND, John	1800	6-296

JAMES, Amos	1847	21-498	JENKINS, William	1843	19-254
		& 462	JENNETT, John B.	1820	11- 99
George	1791	5- 15	JENNINGS, Hannah	1838	16-445
Henrietta	1820	11-171	James	1812	9-255
Henry	1818	10-442	Solomon	1800	6-298
Jane C.	1834	15-194	William	1784	4- 1
John	1788	4-294	JEPHSON, John	1814	9-486
Micajah	1781	3-431	JESSOP, Abraham	1839	17-220
Samuel	1826	12-290	Charles	1828	13- 57
Thomas	1811	9-130	James	1836	15-461'
Thomas	1812	9-228	Nicholas	1807	8-274
Walter	1751	3-418	Ruth	1822	11-372
Watkins	1754	2- 64	William	1781	3-438
William	1838	14-369	William	1829	13-286
JAMISON, Adam	1795	5-246	JESSUP, Mary	1832	14-205
Joseph	1847	22- 84	JEWKES, Francis	1748	1-448
JANNEY, Joseph	1841	18-422	JOB, Nicholas	1816	10-229
JANNIN, Anna	1816	10-119	JOHNES, Hugh	1727	1-233
JARMAN, Benjamin	1812	9-230	JOHNS, Abraham	1731	1-268
John	1792	5- 49	Aquilla	1817	10-379
Robert	1722	1-216	Hannah	1818	10-509
JARRETT, Bennet	1813	9-354	Kinsey	1846	21-132
Emeline	1840	18- 37	Richard	1757	2-225
Rachel	1825	12-163	Richard	1806	8- 29
JARROTT, Abraham	1757	2-236	Richard	1847	21-367
JARVIS, Hannah	1837	16-276	Susan H.	1825	12-106
John R.	1845	20-459	JOHNSON, Alexander	1804	7-305
Osman	1835	15-243	Ann	1803	7-218
JEAN, Mary	1845	21-130	Ann	1807	8-147
JEFFERIES, James	1824	12- 46	Anthony	1721	1-501
JEFFERIS, Samuel	1810	10-417	Barnett	1771	3-195
JEFFERS, John	1797	5-501	Charles	1832	14-183
JEFFERSON, Hamilton	1821	11-260	Christopher	1819	10-586
JEFFERY, Richard	1805	7-358	Daniel	1715	1-117
JENKINS, Ann	1841	18-180	Edward	1797	6- 57
Benedict I.	1838	16-433	Eliza	1847	21-393
Edward	1833	14-321	Elizabeth	1820	11-194
Felix	1838	17- 32	Elizabeth	1835	15-392
Francis I.	1833	14-363	Grafton	1837	16-285
Ignatius	1793	5-105	Israell	1750	2- 35
Job	1833	14-369	James	1840	18- 47
Josias	1823	11-572	Jeremiah	1814	9-495
Louis F.	1840	18-117	Joseph	1731	1-252
Michael	1802	6-523	Joseph	1822	11-367
Richard	1734	2-199	Joshua	1811	9-103
Theresa	1817	10-309	Mary	1814	9-503
Thomas C.	1834	15-205	Mary	1840	18- 98
Thomas C.	1757	2-236	Mary Ann	1820	11-119
William	1721	1-519	Matthew	1815	10- 15
William	1750	2-258	Peter	1831	14-111

JOHNSON, Samuel	1810	9- 18
Samuel	1844	19-499
Thomas	1767	3- 63
Thomas	1791	5- 8
Thomas	1829	13-305
William	1741	1-385
William	1795	5-308
William	1804	7-313
William	1833	14-284
William, Jr.	1767	3- 71
JOHNSTONE, Johannes	1807	8-234
JOICE, Caroline	1846	21-247
JOLLY, Claude	1821	11-331
JONCHURE, Francis I. L.	1824	12- 76
JONES, Andrew D.	1846	21-257
Ann	1759	2-308
Anne	1764	2-163
Benjamin	1739	1-309
Benjamin	1780	3-423
Charles	1840	18- 89
David	1850	23=362
Elizabeth	1840	18- 3
Elizabeth	1847	22- 41
Elizabeth	1848	22-244
Evan	1765	3- 20
Flora	1837	16-383
George	1819	10-610
Henry	1804	7-259
Hester	1787	4-254
Jacob	1838	16-466
James	1839	17-240
John	1785	4- 91
John	1815	10- 88
Jonas	1837	16-226
Joseph	1850	23-434
Joshua	1811	9- 81
Mary	1832	14-236
Mary	1846	21-279
Mary A.	1842	19- 63
Nicholas	1791	5- 6
Philip	1762	2-121
Richard	1737	1-290
Richard	1770	3-161
Richard	1791	4-523
Richard H.	1833	14-337
Robert	1795	5-340
Robinson	1796	5-375
Roger	1815	10- 27
Samuel, Sr.	1849	23- 8
Samuel G.	1842	19- 79
Talbot	1834	14-483

JONES, Theophilus	1735	1-279
Thomas	1675	1- 4
Thomas	1742	1-339
Thomas	1812	9-268
Thomas	1830	13-492
Washington	1830	13-378
William	1773	3-253
William	1816	10-157
William	1830	13-356
William	1839	17-228
JORDAN, Frederick	1813	9-320
John	1816	10-165
John	1824	12- 12
Margaret	1847	22- 72
JORDON, Frederick	1834	15-212
George H.	1842	19-176
John	1795	5-282
Thomas	1835	15-237
William H.	1825	12-118
JOUBERT, James N. H.	1843	19-451
JOURDAN, Edward	1709	1- 21
JUDAH, Abraham	1819	11-16
Manuel	1834	15-156
JUDY, John	1819	10-566
JUES, James	1704	1-68
JUNEA, Bernard	1808	8-364
JUSTICE, Joseph	1801	6-381
JUSTIN, Ann	1813	9-366
JUSTIS, Norton	1832	14-145
KAFFMAN, John	1830	13-444
KAHN, Daniel	1794	5-158
KALBFUS, Lewis	1840	18- 64
Susannah E.	1847	21-492
William	1830	13-349
KANE, Archibald	1818	10-432
KANTZ, Jacob	1811	9-160
Michael	1814	9-401
KAREY, Andrew	1786	3-169
KARNITZICK, Vincent	1823	11-556
KARTHAUS, Charles W.	1843	19-198
Peter A.	1841	18-429
KAUFFMAN, Abraham	1848	22-260
Christian	1812	9-283
KEATINGE, Henry S.	1834	15- 63
KEAVINS, Isabelle	1846	21-302
		& 356
Samuel	1843	19-328
KEEFER, Joseph	1822	11-461
KEEN, Timothy	1733	2-293

KEENE, Zachariah	1834	15- 78
KEENER, Christian	1817	10=384
Jacob	1820	11-100
Melchor	1798	6-129
Melchor	1819	10-609
Peter	1803	7-220
Susannah	1829	13-288
KEEPER, William	1757	2-247
KEERE, Henry	1827	12-386
KEILHOLTZ, Henry	1848	22-318
John	1807	8-208
KEIRLE, Ann	1844	20-215
William H.	1841	18-449
KEISLER, Christopher	1783	3-491
KEITH, William	1810	9- 40
KELBAUGH, Charistian, Jr.		
	1829	13-172
Susanna	1830	13-426
		& 510
KELIHER, Thomas	1805	8- 16
KELLER, Christian	1848	22-368
Jacob	1830	13-442
John	1813	9-290
KELLEY, Charlotte	1815	10- 8
Delilah	1844	20-105
James	1819	10-563
John	1836	16- 44
KELLY, Andrew	1796	5-389
Edward L.	1837	16-413
James	1780	3-397
James	1819	11- 1
Mary	1840	18-150
Michael	1800	6-262
Michael	1817	10-325
Owen	1843	19-432
Susan B.	1834	14-444
Thomas	1773	3-249
Thomas	1830	13-468
Thomas D.	1822	11-373
William	1796	5-425
William	1841	18-305
KELLOGG, Amoss	1843	19-257
KELPS, John	1796	5-434
KELSEY, William	1823	11-602
KELSO, George	1807	8-265
John	1850	23-492
		& 496
Mary	1835	15-223
KEMBELL, John	1705	1- 45
KEMP, James	1827	12-418
John	1686	1- 56

KEMP, John	1823	11-557
Richard	1725	1-226
Richard	1736	1-284
KENNEDAY, Areanah	1804	7-292
KENNEDY, James	1822	11=418
Lawrence	1815	10- 16
Robert	1804	7-225
Thomas	1798	6- 81
Thomas	1849	23-225
KENNY, George	1819	11- 9
Martin	1835	15-411
KENT, Caesar	1810	9- 62
Emanuel	1818	10-470
KENWORTHY, Rebecca	1837	16-380
William	1828	13- 46
KEPPER, Vincent	1795	5-332
KERBY, Dr. Benjamin	1784	3-594
Nicholas	1800	8- 71
KERLINGER, Conrad	1798	6-138
Conrad	1826	12-282
George	1811	9-120
Susanna	1814	9-505
KERR, Archibald	1839	17-288
Eleanor	1816	10-223
James	1808	8-344
James	1834	14-410
John	1810	9- 56
KERSEY, Nicholas	1841	18-197
KESSLER, Ernst F.	1840	18-131
KETCHPOLE, Elizabeth	1818	10-519
KETTIER, Henry	1801	6-357
KEY, Catherine	1848	22-345
Elizabeth W.	1832	14-242
KEYS, Charles	1780	3-406
Charles	1784	3-591
KEYSOR, Derick	1839	17-229
Samuel	1839	17-419
KIAR, Daniel	1836	15-464
KIDD, James	1846	21- 65*
Joshua	1813	9-356
Henry	1783	3-530*
Henry	1847	21-434*
KILGOUR, James	1808	8-327
KILMAN, Levin	1840	18-144
KILPATRICK, John	1834	15-143
John	1848	22-172
Mary	1844	20- 54
KIMBERLY, William H.	1821	11-272
KIMBLE, Hannah	1764	2-175
John	1757	2-241
Robert	1769	3-129

LA ROCHE, Margaretta	1825	12- 83		LEE, George	1843	19-401	
LAROWET, Nicholas	1807	8-196		James	1732	1-260	
LARSCH, Abraham	1810	8-477		John	1676	1-178	
Rebecca	1847	22- 86		John	1831	14- 83	
Valentine	1781	3-428		Mary	1817	10-292	
LASH, George	1821	11-289		Michael	1810	9- 35	
LATIMER, Catherine	1820	11-173		Robert	1827	12-397	
Sturman	1804	7-266		LEEF, John	1836	15-455	
LATOURANDAIS, Philip E.	1832	14-273		LEEKE, Nicholas	1824	11-631	
LATROBE, Margaret	1831	14- 4		LEGARDE, Mary	1820	11-101	
LATY, Joseph	1843	19-432		LEGATT, John	1756	2-111	
LAUDECKER, Simon	1798	6- 78		LEGOE, Benjamin	1759	2-312	
LAUDEMAN, Edward	1847	21-334		LE LACHEUR, William	1836	15-452	
Margaret	1801	6-411		LEINHART, Henry	1825	12-124	
LAUDERMARY, George	1794	5-162		LEITNER, Ignatius	1831	14- 77	
LAUDERSLAGER, Philip	1798	6- 82		LELOUP, Louis F.	1821	11-261	
LAURENS, Roluff	1833	14-340		LEMMON, Alexis	1786	4-151	
LAVATE, Couturier C. A. M.				Fanny P.	1837	16-412	
	1825	12-201		Hannah	1840	18- 91	
LAVELY, Catherine	1803	7-174		Hester	1819	10-608	
William	1787	4-263		Jacob	1797	6- 59	
LAW, Catherine	1848	22-352		Jacob	1815	10- 76	
		& 437		John	1811	9-113	
George	1848	22-471		Richard	1796	5-392	
LAWLESS, Matthew	1849	23-137		Richard	1849	23-126	
LAWRENCE, Daniel	1781	3-433		Sarah	1812	9-261	
John	1782	3-481		Sarah	1823	11-554	
John	1798	6-126		Susanna	1811	9-166	
Joseph	1797	5-483		LENNOX, Sarah	1819	10-567	
Richard	1833	14-326		LENOX, Ruth	1790	4-385	
LAWSON, Alexander	1761	2-337		William	1724	1-209	
Alexander	1798	6-136		William A.	1836	16- 84	
Elizabeth	1814	9-411		LEONARD, Joseph	1820	11-103	
George	1823	11-613		LEPPO, Jacob	1801	6-398	
Richard	1830	13-343		LEREW, Francis	1811	9- 83	
LAYPOLD, Charles	1788	4-292		LEROY, Manguen	1799	6-207	
LEACH, Shepherd	1834	14-429		LESOURD, John	1822	11-461	
LEAGUE, Ann	1811	9- 86		LESTER, Ann	1749	1-454	
Aquilla	1801	6-395		William	1811	9-172	
Eleanor	1781	3-425		LETTER, Thomas	1823	11-502	
Luke	1784	4- 32		LEVOI, Thomas	1820	11-180	*
LEARY, Cornelius	1784	4- 10		LEVERING, Enoch	1795	5-329	
LEASIE, Margaret	1757	2-240		Enoch	1828	13- 54	
LEBRANTHWAITE, James A.				Jesse	1832	14-228	
	1847	21-327		Nathan	1834	15- 51	
LECLERC, Francis	1822	11-377		Susan	1839	15-358	
LECOMPTE, Nehemiah	1773	3-245		LEVILLIAN, Michael	1832	14-200	*
LEDGER, John	1775	3-310		LEVY, Hetty	1816	10-155	
LEDLEY, Jacob	1850	23-422		Nathan	1846	21- 76	
LEE, George	1816	10-168		Rachel	1794	5-216	

LEWIN, Samuel	1784	4- 24	LITTLE, Thomas	1764	2-165
LEWIS, Anna M.	1835	15-377	LITTLEJOHN, Miles	1816	10-103
David	1812	9-206	Sarah	1839	17-344
Elizabeth	1814	9-409	Thomas	1841	14- 15
Ephraim	1818	10-529	LITTLER, Isaiah	1826	12-268
Henry	1806	8-132	LITZINGER, George	1811	9-147
James H.	1841	18-244	Henry	1828	13- 28
John	1784	3-576	LIVERS, Anthony	1820	11-165
John	1836	16- 55	LIVES, Rosetta	1848	22-261
Joseph	1769	3-132	LIVINGSTON, John	1838	16-465
Lewis D.	1829	13-177	LLOYD, John	1836	16-147
Nathan	1777	3-353	Peregrine	1800	6-313
Nicholas	1819	10-590	Thomas	1814	9-456
Nicholas	1828	13-114	LOANE, Edward	1845	20-484
Thomas	1822	11-469	LOBB, Joseph	1724	1-212
William	1826	12-218	LOCK, William	1786	4-138
LEYPOLD, Frederick	1821	11-288	LOCKARD, Thomas	1830	13-414
John	1810	9- 14	LOCKERS, William	1790	4-483
LIDDICK, Philip	1779	3-387	LOCKETT, John	1704	1- 76
LIGHTHIZER, Joshua	1837	16-292	LOCKS, John	1842	19- 40
LIGHTNER, George	1815	9-521	LOGAN, Michael	1813	9-335
LILLY, Asaph	1825	12-217	LOGUE, Edward	1849	23-306
Eli	1847	22-116	James	1846	21-112
LIMEBERGER, Andrew	1804	7-284	William	1846	21- 57
LINBERGER, Susanna	1837	16-246	LOMAX, Caleb	1825	12-170
William	1832	14-241	LONEY, John	1765	3- 35
LINCH, Abarila	1767	3- 72	LONG, David	1791	5- 30
Dr. Cornelius	1768	3- 99	Elizabeth	1845	20-390
Eleanor	1760	2-266	James	1807	8-170
Robuck	1716	1-229	Jane	1696	1- 50
LINDENBERGER, George	1796	5- 39	John	1759	2-311
George	1820	11-185	Kennedy	1824	11-641
Rebecca	1850	23-368	Mary	1783	3-526
Susanna	1812	9-255	Robert	1779	3-389
LINDSAY, John	1801	6-422	Robert	1808	8-330
Robert	1805	7-405	Robert C.	1833	14-299
LING, Robert	1831	14- 33	Samuel	1817	10-279
LINGAN, Susan	1844	20-176	Thomas	1823	11-597
LINGENFELTER, Jacob	1815	10- 28	Thomas	1824	11-662
LIPPINCOTT, Catherine	1849	23- 15	William C.	1815	10- 80
LITCHE, Jacob	1788	4-296	LONGLAND, Richard	1709	1- 24
LITTEN, Thomas	1761	2-342	LOUDENSLAGER, George	1823	11-617
LITTIG, Philip	1836	16-120	Jacob	1822	11-375
LITTLE, George	1757	2-245	LOVALL, Henry	1829	13-180
Guy	1764	2-182	LOVE, Elizabeth	1815	10- 14
Jacob	1825	12-149	John	1709	1- 37
John	1774	3-298	Kitura	1847	21-357
Ludwick	1826	12-303	Martha	1846	21- 82
Mary C.	1835	15-297	Miles	1786	4-142
Peter	1830	13-374	Robert	1692	1- 79

LOVE, Thomas	1821	11-229	LYNCH, Ann	1825	12-248
William	1708	1- 22	Anthony	1837	16-257
LOVEALL, Ethan	1795	5-298	Elizabeth	1837	16-321
Luther	1821	11-211	John	1797	5-480
Zebulon	1786	4-118	John	1848	22-157
LOVEDON, Thomas	1798	6-149	Joshua	1844	20-159
LOVELACE, Francis	1684	1- 52	Patrick	1766	3- 52
LOVELL, William	1842	19- 15	Patrick	1803	7-169
LOVERING, William	1813	9-331	Robuck	1797	5-504
LOW, John	1789	3-401	Robuck	1821	11-213
Joseph	1837	16-202	William	1799	6-152
Joshua	1808	8-361	William	1800	6-251
LOWE, David	1839	17-443	William	1806	8-131
Hannah	1831	14- 98	LYON, Ann	1832	14-167
John	1816	10-112	James E.	1838	16-499
Nicholas	1823	11-622	James	1841	18-273
Margaret	1849	23-299	John	1840	18- 82
William	1743	1-346	Joseph S.	1839	17-172
William	1826	12-257	Robert	1842	19- 3
LOWCOCK, Thomas	1756	2-115	Robert, Jr.	1845	20-337
LOWMAN, Emory	1837	16-288	Samuel H.	1842	19- 86
LOWNSBURY, John	1792	5- 47	William	1794	5-185
LOWRE, Jein	1817	10-390	LYONS, Jane	1847	21-407
LOWRY, Margaret	1840	18-122	LYTFOOT, Thomas	1687	1- 71
Robert	1820	11-193	LYTLE, James	1809	8-386
William	1836	16- 91	James	1818	10-484
LOYD, Elizabeth	1748	1-420			
John	1743	1-351			
LUCAS, Basil	1803	7-196	McALISTER, Alexander	1806	8- 96
Henry	1843	19-459	McALLISTER, James	1796	5-346
James	1820	11-111	John	1839	17-252
Priscilla	1826	12-272	John	1839	17-367
Thomas	1819	11- 63	Joseph	1784	3-560
Thomas	1832	14-226	Lloyd	1837	16-334
LUKENS, Joseph	1826	16-152	Monora	1815	9-518
LUSBY, Joseph	1764	2-172	Richard	1802	7-105
LUSHRO, Ann M.	1819	11- 57	Robert	1784	4- 22
LUTGEN, Catherine	1820	11-157	McAVOY, Hugh	1847	22-117
LUX, Agnes	1783	3-496	McBEAN, Angus	1815	10- 86
Ann	1785	4- 43	McCABE, Edward	1814	9-435
Catherine	1790	4-417	Hugh	1836	15-485
Darby	1750	2- 25	John	1838	17- 1
Darby	1812	9-281	McCALL, Jean	1761	2-340
George	1797	6- 18	McCANDLESS, George	1793	5- 82
Mary	1813	9-329	McCAN, Timothy	1757	2-242
Rachel	1813	9-294	McCANN, John B.	1846	21-190
William	1778	3-357	William	1836	15-486
William	1825	12-163	McCANNON, Ann	1838	17-153
LYETH, John	1845	20-273	McCARRIER, James	1838	17- 10
Samuel	1817	10-309	McCARTER, William	1818	10-513

McCARTY, Samuel	1773	3-271	McCULLOH, James	1798	6- 72
McCASKEY, Alexander	1798	6- 83	Margaret	1784	4- 26
McCASLIN, Henry	1780	3-409	Samuel	1849	23- 1
McCAULEY, Robert	1849	23-248	McCULLOUGH, Elizabeth	1847	21-427
McCAUSLAND, Jacob	1825	12-185	McCURDY, Hugh	1805	7-381
Marcus	1827	12-405	McCURLEY, Felix, Sr.	1845	20-368
McCLAIN, John	1825	12- 97	McDERMOT, Catherine	1824	11-626
McCLARY, Thomas	1803	7-223	Christopher	1816	10-247
McCLASKEY, James	1833	14-289	McDERMOTT, Charles	1808	8-308
McCLELLAN, Jannet	1826	12-256	William	1843	19-232
Maria	1845	20-309	McDONALD, Alexander	1832	14-138
John	1809	8-368	Alexander	1840	18- 40
McCLUNG, John	1780	3-437	Daniel	1845	20-313
Robert	1784	3-589	James	1832	14-149
Thomas R.	1836	16-10	William	1845	20-430
McCLURE, James	1840	17-472	McDONNELL, John	1810	9- 66
McCOLLISTER, Robert	1817	10-404	McDOWELL, Hamilton	1825	12-181
McCOMAS, Alexander	1761	2-352	William P.	1827	12-391
Aquila	1773	3-247	McELDERRY, Edward	1825	12-153
Daniel	1765	3- 19	Elizabeth	1819	11- 61
Margaret	1818	10-468	John	1830	13-418
Robert A.	1844	20-139	Thomas	1810	9- 5
William	1815	10- 37	McELROY, Matthew	1840	18- 58
McCOMB, John	1831	13-505	Patrick	1847	22- 43
McCOMESKY, Daniel	1790	4-427			& 111
John	1823	11-551	MacENERY, Matthew	1845	20-101
McCONKEY, William	1844	20-212	McFADDON, Neal	1801	6-397
McCONNELL, Robert	1813	9-353	McFADON, Alexander	1782	3-449
McCORKELL, Mary	1846	21- 49	John	1780	3-410
McCORMICK, John	1840	18-139	McFARLAND, Edward	1839	17-197
William	1781	3-431	McFERRAN, Jane	1839	17-268
William	1807	8-185	McFERRAN, John	1827	12-331
McCOY, Andrew	1839	17-295	McGAW, John	1819	10-556
Isaac	1836	15-475	Richard	1845	20-250
Margaret	1837	16-361	Sarah	1803	9-236
Martha	1830	13-383	Sarah	1848	22-177
Robert	1838	16-521	McGEE, Jane	1797	5-491
Thomas (McCove?)	1767	3- 69	McGEOCH, Andrew	1838	16-515
Thomas	1847	22- 85	McGIBBON, James	1836	16-108
McCRACKEN, William	1843	19-399	Tumislion	1843	19-228
McCREDEN, Isaac	1835	15-375	McGILL, Andrew	1764	2-181
McCREERY, Thomas	1796	5-373	McGINNIS, Abigail	1824	12- 74
Thomas	1796	5-484	Eleanor	1842	19-193
McCRISTOL, John	1822	11-466	McGLAGHIN, William	1803	7-139
McCUBBIN, Susan	1838	17-124	McGLENNAN, Mary	1822	11-427
William	1814	9-450	McGOURLEY, John	1845	20-426
McCULLEY, James	1821	11-255	McGREGOR, David	1833	14-382
McCULLOCH, James H.	1836	16-149	McGREGORY, John	1797	5-527
McCULLOH, David	1766	3- 34	McHENRY, Francis D.	1847	21-343
Eleanor	1840	17-473	James	1816	10-174

McHENRY, Margaret	1833	14-400		MacCREARY, William	1814	9-450
McHUGH, Ann	1833	14-334		MACCUBBIN, Ann	1798	6-107
McILVAINE, George	1825	12-171		Samuel	1739	1-321
McINTOSH, James	1824	11-651		Sarah	1799	6-166
Margaret	1815	10- 89		Zachariah	1791	5- 13
McKAY, Gilbert	1838	16-497		MacDONALD, Alexander	1836	16- 80
John	1830	13-480		MACE, Charles R.	1840	18- 57
McKEEL, Thomas	1807	8-270		MacENERY, Matthew	1844	20-101
McKEEN, John	1839	17-435		MACGAVIAN, John	1769	3-111
McKEEVER, John	1849	23-175		MACGILL, Mary	1824	12- 51
McKELDIN, Joseph	1835	15-229		Patrick	1813	9-362
McKENNA, Francis	1797	6- 6		See also pp. 507 and 532		
McKEWEN, John	1833	14-408		MACHER, Benjamin	1824	12- 66
McKIM, Alexander	1832	14-123		MACKELFRESH, David	1819	10-550
David T.	1847	22- 7		Margaret	1841	18-210
Elizabeth	1834	15-100		MACKENHEIMER, Catherine	1829	13-254
John	1819	10-606		Gabriel	1792	5- 39
John, Jr.	1842	18-487		John	1823	11-606
Mary	1828	13-139		Nicholas	1819	10-549
Robert	1819	10-563		Peter	1801	6-441
McKINSEY, Rodrick	1795	5-302		Susanna	1810	9- 10
McKUBBIN, Zachariah	1791	5- 13		MACKEY, Michael	1820	11-153
McLANAHAN, James	1844	20-174		MACKIE, Ebenezer,	1796	5-387
McLAUGHLIN, Mary	1799	6-169		MACLANE, Hector	1722	1-192
Peter	1832	14-234		MACLONE, James	1724	1-211
Thomas	1837	16-251		MACQUAIN, Dugal	1746	1-409
William	1795	5-233		MACTIER, Alexander, Sr.	1831	14-101
McLEAN, Anna M.	1847	22-124		MAGAN, Elizabeth A.	1832	14-259
McLEROY, William	1802	7- 64		MAGAW, Adam	1783	3-490
McLURE, John	1805	7-420		MAGGS, Jane	1832	14-198
McMAHON, Abigail	1807	8-146		MAGIL, Caroline	1807	8-162
McMEAL, Catherine	1836	16-110		MAGINNESS, Sarah	1843	19-320
McMACHIN, David	1810	9- 12		MAGLENEN, James	1821	11-278
Sarah	1849	22-488		MAGRATH, Thomas	1816	10-183
McMURRAY, John	1846	21-143		MAGRUDER, Richard B.	1844	20- 12
McNEAL, Elizabeth	1847	21-492		MAGUIRE, Sarah	1816	10-256
James, Jr.	1831	14-107		MAINSTER, Samuel	1838	16-435
McNEILL, John	1810	9- 65		MAIRANT, Charles L.	1822	11-400
McPHILLIPS, Lemuel	1831	14- 40		MAHOME, John	1741	1-338
McQUINN, William	1823	11-511		MAHON, Edward	1733	1-275
William	1834	15- 36		MALCOM, Hannah	1832	14-189'
McRACEL, George	1796	5-430		Peter	1847	21 -424
McSHERRY, James	1849	23- 31		MALIN, William	1810	8-481
McSWENEY, Paul	1844	20- 41		MALLONEE, Dennis	1844	20- 77
MABEE, Ann	1845	20-324		John	1783	3-536
MACARTNEY, John, Jr.	1824	12- 5		MALLORY, John	1831	14- 22
MACCLAN, William	1752	2- 44		MALLOY, Charles	1829	13-186
MACCOMAS, Aquila	1771	3-178		Patrick	1822	11-468
William	1748	1-425		MALONE, Timothy	1848	22-399
MacCREARY, Letita	1850	23-350		MALTER, Alphonse	1840	18-134

MAN, Anthony	1823	11-597	MARSHALL, Thomas	1778	3-372
Benjamin	1762	2-152	William	1721	1-510
MANCHESTER, Asa	1821	11-227	William	1809	8-441
MANCKEY, Elizabeth	1814	9-434	MARTIN, Ann	1807	8-168
MANN, Frederick	1821	11-329	Edward	1822	11-415
William	1835	15-305	Elizabeth A.	1845	20-323
MANNE, Anthony	1810	9- 30	James	1838	17-114
MANNING, Abraham	1835	15-352	John	1718	1-126
MANNON, Samuel	1803	7-156	John	1783	3-538
MANOUCH, John	1783	3-529	John J.	1806	8- 31
MANUS, Eleanor	1828	13- 21	Patrick	1842	19- 91
Peggy	1806	8-508	Patrick	1846	21-304
MANWARING, Jacob	1797	5- 11	Peachy	1821	11-283
MARBLE, Jane	1836	15-491	Robert	1830	13-442
MARCH, Charles	1766	3- 38	Susan C. I.	1845	20-321
Michael	1820	11-166	MARTINDALE, Ann	1820	11-152
MARCHAND, Pierre	1825	12- 82	MASCHBERGER, David	1807	8-239
MAREC, Elizabeth	1833	14-393	MASEMORE, George	1828	13-136
MARER, John P.	1829	13-330	MASH, Barbara	1831	14- 91
MARGAY, John	1809	8-371	MASON, Elizabeth	1847	22- 70
MARIAS, Joseph	1815	9-512	Francis A.	1849	23-285
MARK, John	1712	1-116	John	1736	1-282
MARKELL, John	1788	4-305	Joseph	1848	22-166
---- ----	1811	9-181	Peter	1844	20- 59
Henry	1837	16-267	Rachel	1837	16-419
Jacob	1822	11-422	MASSEY, Aquila	1739	1-406
John	1824	12- 64	Aquila	1759	1-310
Solomon, Jr.	1830	13-408	Jonathan	1732	1-261
MARLIACQ, John	1847	21-467	Rigbie	1841	18-285
MARLICK, Dembo	1810	8-474	William A.	1825	12- 87
MARQUESS, Thomas	1833	14-280	MASSICOT, William	1847	21-459
MARRIOTT, William	1823	11-548	MATHEWS, George	1776	3-315
MARRISETTE, Peter	1798	6-144	Thomas	1774	3-290
MARSH, Benedict	1832	14-159	William	1806	8-134
Catherine	1847	21-451	MATHEWSON, Asahel	1825	12-170
Dennis	1832	14-249	MATTHEWS, Ann	1822	11-443
John	1807	8-143	Anna	1815	10- 34
Grafton	1825	12-194	Betseyan	1839	17-385
John	1807	8-136	Charlotte	1849	23-269
John	1846	21- 42	Edward	1829	13-285
Joshua	1825	12-189	Edward	1833	14-395
Stephen	1829	13-269	Elizabeth	1748	1-447
Temperance	1849	23-221	Elizabeth	1828	13- 89
MARECHAL, Ambrose	1828	13- 28	Henry	1726	1-224
MARSCHALL, Francis	1841	18-214	James	1760	2-254
MARSEILLE, Joseph	1846	21-308	James	1840	18-135
MARSELIAS, Andres	1807	8-134	John	1835	15-419
MARSHALL, James	1784	4- 8	Leah	1793	5-104
James	1797	6- 33	Mordecai	1830	15-380
Mary	1749	1-365	Nicholas	1820	11-128

INDEX OF BALTIMORE COUNTY WILLS

MATTHEWS, Oliver	1824	11-626	MERCER, Luke	1775	3-305
Patrick	1809	8-457	MERCIER, Richard	1816	10-197
Peter	1824	12- 51	MEREDITH, Joshua	1821	11-304
Roger	1789	1- 22	Samuel	1825	12-188
Roger	1741	1-377	Thomas	1840	18- 22
Samuel	1842	19-173	MERICA, George	1828	13- 32
Thomas	1792	5- 34	MERIDITH, Benjamin	1803	7-182
William	1819	11- 76	Samuel	1785	4- 54
William	1819	11- 78	MERRIKEN, Elizabeth	1834	15-184
William	1821	11-225	Joshua	1726	1-234
MATTHOIT, Christian	1816	10-125	Joshua	1811	9-198
MATTINGLY, William	1746	1-444	MERRYMAN, Avarilla	1785	4- 60
MATTOX, John	1774	3-286	Benjamin	1796	5-381
William	1804	7-341	Benjamin	1814	9-465
MAUREAN, Ann U. P.	1850	23-357	Caleb	1825	12- 85
MAURET, Francis	1830	13-422	Charles	1722	1-189
MAXWELL, Assael	1727	2-195	Capt. Charles	1725	1-221
David	1756	2-101	Elijah	1799	6-192
Elizabeth	1829	13-246	Elijah	1840	18- 34
James	1727	1-215	George	1823	11-591
John	1762	2-139	Jane	1819	11- 80
Mary	1823	11-546	John	1749	1-458
Robert	1813	9-288	John	1777	3-352
MAY, Benjamin	1811	9- 84	John	1801	6-415
Benjamin	1847	22- 92	John	1814	9-417
MAYDWELL, Alexander	1804	7-288	John	1841	18-317
MAYER, Isaac	1817	10-290	John, of Benj.	1849	23-291
MAYNARD, Juliana	1846	21-127	Joseph	1799	6-159
MAYNOR, John	1770	3-164	Joshua	1801	6-353
MEAD, Benjamin	1830	13-360	Martha	1801	6-390
Joseph	1737	1-292	Martico	1807	8-262
Martha	1810	8-505	Micajah, Sr.	1842	19- 89
Patrick	1817	10-361	Nicholas	1787	4-271
William	1793	5-130	Nicholas	1770	3-163
MEADS, Benedict	1840	18- 94	Nicholas	1801	6-443
Benjamin	1764	2-177	Nicholas	1802	6-504
Edward	1763	2-364			& 514
Joshua	1820	11-107	Nicholas	1816	10-118
Manas	1814	9-504	Samuel	1787	4-283
MEDCALF, Abigail	1845	21- 16	Samuel	1754	2- 55
MEDINGER, John J.	1843	19-344	Samuel, Jr.	1805	8- 1
MEEDS, Mary	1835	15-330	Samuel	1810	8-469
MEETEER, William	1833	14-336	Sarah	1816	10-216
MEHLHORN, Casper	1834	15-203	Thomas	1820	11-647
MELEM, John	1676	1- 70	William	1805	7-387
MELLOR, Charles	1841	18-383	William, Jr.	1823	11-506
MENCHI, Anthony	1834	15-123	MERSSER, William	1759	2-303
MENGER, George P.	1795	5-275	MESSERSMITH, Frances	1840	18- 27
MERCER, John	1777	3-349	George	1802	7- 8

MESSONNIER, Henry	1823	11-541	MILLER, Lewis	1848	22-373
METGER, Conrad	1804	7-339	Matilda	1829	13-222
METZ, John	1842	19- 18	Michael	1834	15- 58
MEWSHAW, Rachel	1848	22-418	Nicholas	1782	3-459
MEYER, Andrew	1848	22-362	Nicholas	1809	8-404
Godfrey	1848	22-347	Robert	1834	15- 32
MEYERS, Balser	1772	3-228	Robert, Jr.	1849	23- 6
MIARS, Lawrence	1788	4-306	Susannah	1836	15- 13
MICHAEL, Wendel	1821	11-306	Thomas	1814	9-501
MIDDLEMORE, Frances	1759	2-298	MILLERON, Jacob	1818	10-488
Dr. Josias	1755	1-485	MILLS, George	1822	11-383
MIDDLETON, Gilbert	1827	12-329	MILLAIN, Henry	1737	1-293
William	1805	7-408	MILLWARD, William	1780	3-407
MILANDER, Thomas	1798	6-141	MILTENBERGER, Catherine		
MILDRED, Daniel	1788	4-331		1834	15-159
MILES, Aquila	1808	8-293	George	1797	6- 55
Jane	1843	19-251	MINCE, Joseph	1839	17-437
Thomas	1766	3- 74	MINCHIN, Frederick B.	1829	13-255
Thomas	1831	14- 30	John	1802	7- 1
MILHAW, Michael	1816	10-123	MINGO, John	1811	9-169
MILHUSE, Bartholomew	1743	1-350	MITCHELL, Ann Jane	1816	10-159
MILLARD, Joseph L.	1824	11-624	Barbara	1807	8-278
MILLDEWS, Elizabeth	1805	7-379	Charles	1831	14- 58
MILLIRON, Mary	1840	17-470	Elizabeth A.	1841	18-330
MILLEM, Moses	1830	13-460	Francis I.	1825	12-106
MILLER, Alexander	1800	6-312	Hannah	1831	14- 43
Alexander	1820	11-155	John	1822	11-350
Araminta	1843	19-296	John P.	1807	8-195
Charles	1827	12-406	Peter	1805	7-442
Eli	1829	13-265	MOALE, Ellin	1825	12-111
Elijah	1823	11-601	George W.	1799	6-176
Elizabeth	1800	6-341	John	1740	1-325
Elizabeth	1816	10-120	John	1798	6-114
Emily	1832	14-190	Richard	1786	4-133
George	1817	10-377	Richard	1802	7- 92
George W.	1836	15-483	Thomas	1832	14-271
Hannah	1833	14-448	MOELIN, Charles D.	1802	7- 27
Hugh	1789	4-391	MOFFETT, Louisa	1805	7-421
Jacob	1829	13-292	MOFFIT, John	1818	10-523
Jacob	1833	14-290	Olivia	1829	13-249
James	1799	6-206	MOFFITT, Thomas	1850	23-450
Jane	1841	18-189	MOHAN, Barbara	1817	10-363
Johanna	1785	4- 66	MOHLAR, Jacob	1773	3-272
John	1785	4- 88	MOHLER, Elizabeth	1787	4-265
John	1799	6-179	MONDEL, Catherine	1836	16-126
John	1800	6-297	MONDELL, William	1819	10-600
John	1816	10-237	MONEA, Nephrey	1811	9-153
John	1836	16- 87	MONK, George	1837	16-411
Joseph	1799	6-201	Renaldo	1769	3-123
Joseph	1801	6-475	MONKS, Catherine	1826	12-241

MONTGOMERY, Mary	1841	18-334	MORRIS, John	1829	13-238
Sidney	1843	19-459	John	1834	15-104
Stewart	1847	21-391	Joseph	1843	19-336
MOODY, William	1808	8-318	Margaret	1834	15- 86
William	1834	15- 88	otherwise called Margaret		
MOONEY, Margaret S.	1845	20-483	Murray		
Patrick	1849	23-242	Owen	1831	14- 97
Richard	1821	11-305	Thomas	1835	15-406
MOORAN, Daniel	1819	11- 29	William	1800	6-300
MOORE, Ann	1792	5- 62	MORROW, James	1809	8-380
Delia	1849	23-244	Thomas	1800	6-326
Hannah	1785	4-104	MORSE, Abraham	1806	8- 51
Henry	1848	22-187	Robert C.	1849	23- 60
James	1808	8-346	MORTHLAND, Michael	1815	10- 69
James	1820	11-164	Sarah	1846	21-156
James	1838	17- 31	Robert	1838	16-514
John	1761	2-333	MORTIMER, James M.	1814	9-502
John	1847	21-440	Thomas	1828	13-,92
Mary	1783	3-496	MORTON, Maria W.	1844	20- 36
Nathan H. T.	1844	20- 39	William	1751	3-416
Nathaniel	1816	10-111	MOSCHBERGER, David	1799	6-206
Nicholas R.	1816	10-232	MOSHER, James	1845	20-293
Peggy	1844	19-484	MOSHO, Christena	1840	18- 48
Robert	1787	4-276	MOSS, Bridget	1843	19-463
Stephen	1782	3-448	Charles	1826	12-316
Thomas	1820	11-207	MOTHERLY, Charles	1786	4-188
Walter	1783	3-450	MOTHLAND, Samuel	1813	9-298
William	1776	3-329	MOTT, Gershom	1772	3-209
William	1837	16-308	MOTTE, Francis	1846	21- 58
William	1824	12- 75	MOUK, Henry	1803	7-165
		& 76	MOULE, Joseph	1802	7- 45
William	1841	18-381	MOULTON, Matthew	1725	1-225
MORDIERE, Theresa	1817	10-323	MOUNT, Barney	1836	16- 76
MORE, Samuel	1845	20-427	MOUTALIBER, Martha G. P.		
MOREL, John B.	1848	22-463		1826	12-252
MORGAN, David	1802	7- 80	MOUNTGOMERY, Patrick	1759	2-313
David	1771	3-182	MOWTON, James	1850	23-446
Hugh	1749	1-468	MUDIE, Jane	1783	3-551
James	1802	7- 35	MULL, Michael	1773	3-270
Michael	1837	16-342	MULLER, Elizabeth A.	1821	11-251
Nicholas	1824	12- 79	George C.	1817	10-328
Thomas	1697	1-179	MULLIKIN, Richard D.	1815	10- 93
MORIANGES, Etienne	1804	7-270	MULLIN, Thomas, Sr.	1848	22-462
MORPHEBOUS, Henry	1824	12- 61	William	1785	4- 94
MORRAY, James	1704	1- 91	MUMA, Abraham	1789	4-367
MORREN, James	1844	20-142	MUMMA, Christian	1831	14- 68
MORRIS, Alexander	1849	23-164	David	1791	5- 17
Belinda	1826	12-240	David	1816	10-242
Edward	1833	14-284	George	1836	15-451
Jacob	1735	2-200	MUMMY, John	1813	9-302

MUNCKS, Andrew	1836	16-114		MYERS, Philip	1812	9-273
MUNDAY, Edward	1757	2-246		Philip	1830	13-437
Hannah	1757	2-233		William	1838	17-113
Leah	1840	18-133		MYLES, Jane	1843	19-408
William	1830	13-341		Zachary	1842	19- 1
MUMMINGS, Shadrack	1797	6- 44				
MUNROE, Elizabeth	1845	20-475				
MUNSON, Ann	1835	15-346		NACE, Adam	1821	11-254
MUNTROP, Lalewg	1847	21-416		Bernard	1829	13-206
MUNZ, Mathias	1848	22-406		George	1809	8-373
MURPHY, Charles	1784	4- 25		Mary	1825	12- 98
Eleanor	1820	11-168		Peter	1831	14-108
John	1729	1-242		NAGLE, Catherine	1843	19-339
John	1842	19-125		Henry	1820	11- 97
William	1768	3- 88		NAGOT, Francis C.	1831	14- 99
William	1804	7-268		NANCE, Rowland	1683	1- 71
William	1820	11-200		NANTS, John	1825	12-164
MURRAY, Ann	1846	21-275		NANTZ, John G.	1848	22-327
Christopher	1828	13- 69		NAPPETT, Samuel	1808	8-328
Edward	1794	5-202		NARGUN, Magness	1807	8-193
Frances	1843	19-352		NASH, William	1848	22-141
James	1704	1- 91		NATTALI, Othriel	1818	10-429
John	1785	4- 81		NAYLOR, John	1796	5-451
John	1816	10-218		NEAL, Barbara	1834	15- 70
John	1833	14-296		Hugh	1812	9-205
John	1832	14-276		John	1819	10-583
Josephus	1772	3-216		Richard	1842	19- 42
Margaret	1834	15- 86		NEALE, Abner	1824	12- 36
Peter	1840	18- 6		Bennett	1803	7-194
Rose	1805	7-380		NEAVITT, Mary A.	1843	19-430
Ruth	1782	3-449		NEEDHAM, Ann I.	1849	23-298
Sarah	1847	22-133		Asa H.	1849	23- 86
Thomas	1828	13-127		NEFF, Abraham	1784	3-557
Wheeler	1816	10-135		Henry	1796	5-388
MUSGRAVE, George	1847	21-475		Henry	1830	13-387
MYER, John J.	1841	18-459		NEILL, William	1785	4- 53
Thomas	1848	22-250		NEILSON, Ann	1834	14-435
MYERS, Arthur	1844	20- 28		Deborah	1831	14- 83
Barbara	1823	11-540		Harriet W.	1846	21-169
Elizabeth	1830	13-333		Jane	1801	6-429
Frederick	1786	4-182		John	1810	9- 39
Henry	1821	11-294		Joseph	1840	18- 15
Jacob	1787	4-268		Robert	1799	6-168
Jacob	1845	21- 20		Robert	1850	23-433
Jacob	1847	23- 12		Robert D.	1827	12-385
James	1836	16-157		Samuel	1840	18- 43
John	1845	20-238		Susanna C.	1806	8- 39
Margaret	1804	7-309		NELMS, George P.	1840	18-105
Maria A.	1842	18-482		NELSON, Benjamin	1784	3-590
Nicholas	1840	18- 24		Burgess	1791	4-534

NELSON, Francis	1740	1-330		NORRIS, Benjamin	1772	3-229
Isabella	1841	18-248		Edward	1763	3- 3
James	1817	10-345		John	1761	2-328
John	1789	4-387		John	1787	4-202
NENNINGER, John	1839	17-175		Joseph	1784	4- 31
NEVINS, William	1835	15-384		Kezia	1828	13- 98
NEWHAUS, Carsten	1816	10-187		Margaret	1847	21-362
NEWMAN, Catherine	1831	14- 21		Mordecai	1849	23-104
Harriet	1847	21-423		Thomas	1761	2-357
Jacob	1834	14-433		Thomas	1827	12-384
Jane	1847	21-359		William	1720	1-163
John	1733	2-288		William	1833	14-293
Lawson	1839	17-307		William, Jr.	1819	10-552
Nathaniel	1821	11-225		William E.	1809	8-379
Roger	1704	1- 35		NORTH, John	1699	1-173
NEWTON, Isaac	1822	11-462		Robert	1749	1-411
NICE, David	1782	3-475		NORTON, John	1727	1-231
NICHOLSON, Benjamin	1792	5- 46		NORWOOD, Edward	1772	3-200
Benjamin	1837	16-213'		Elizabeth H.	1848	22-396
John	1844	20-106		Henrietta H.	1849	23-122
Joseph	1787	4-252		John	1823	11-507
Mary	1804	7-300		John	1827	12-416
Mary	1810	9- 72		Mary	1822	11-497
Matilda H.	1805	7-368		Mary A.	1841	18-328
Ruth	1791	5- 12		Nicholas	1786	4-168
William	1761	2-346		Samuel	1773	3-263
NICOLAI, Ludwig H. W.	1849	23-307		Samuel	1815	10- 1
NICHOL, Alexander	1793	5- 79		NOYES, William M.	1836	16-101
NICOLLS, William	1829	13-325		NULL, Jacob	1812	9-275
NICOLS, Charlotte	1843	19-385		NULTY, Mary	1847	21-392
Henry	1831	13-506		NURSE, Rufus	1826	12-307
NICHOLS, James B.	1828	13- 85		NUSSUM, Thomas	1720	1-517
Margaret	1787	4-258		NUTON, John	1674	1- 7
Peggy	1849	22-490		NUTZ, Sarah A.	1848	22-240
NICOIS, Sarah	1829	13-305				
NICOLLS, Stephen	1794	5-286				
NILES, Hezekiah	1839	17-281		OATES, William K.	1801	6-404
NIPPERT, Elizabeth	1824	11-637		OBERHOFF, Frederick	1825	12- 99*
George	1815	9-522		O'BRIEN, Charles C. C.	1839	17-401
NOBLE, William	1732	1-264		James	1800	6-285
NOEL, Septimus	1794	5-160		Matthew	1815	10- 73
Sarah	1847	21-353		O'BIER, Sally	1821	11-257*
NOELKER, Ehrenfried	1808	8-348		O'CONNOR, Catherine	1840	18-104
NOLL, Anthony	1801	6-347		John	1819	11- 57
NOLTE, John M.	1834	15-157		ODELL, Isaiah	1847	21-395
NOON, William	1789	4-359		John	1818	10-427
NORBURY, George	1823	11-537		Walter	1828	13- 75
NORMAN, George	1697	1-172		O'DONNELL, Elliott	1837	16-274
NORRIS, Abraham	1802	6-550		Hugh	1814	9-506
Ann	1841	18-267		John	1805	7-448

O'DONNELL, Mary	1848	22-257	OSBORN, James	1798	6- 97
OGDEN, Amos	1818	10-419	Joseph	1823	11-558
Mary	1818	10-440	William	1704	1-140
OGG, Benjamin	1821	11-327	OTTERBEIN, William	1813	9-373
Francis	1733	2-292	OTTEY, William	1773	3-277
George	1770	3-121	OTTO, George H.	1812	9-231
Hellin	1798	6- 92	OURSLER, Edward	1795	5-244
Laban	1832	14-152	OUTZ, Peter	1820	11-123
Mary	1846	21- 49	OWEN, Mary	1846	21-167
OGIER, John W.	1800	6-273	OWENS, Samuel	1847	23- 50
OGLEBY, James	1823	11-582	William	1831	14- 21
O'HEARE, John	1835	15-252	OWINGS, Bale	1782	3-455
O'KEEFEE, Daniel	1835	15-380	Bale	1831	14- 16
OKERMAN, Christiona	1789	4-344	Beale	1822	11-334
O'LAUGHLEN, Michael	1843	19-420	Beale	1843	19-366
OLDDEN, David	1806	8-133	Caleb	1816	10-138
OLDEN, George I.	1825	12-100	Christopher	1783	3-516
O'LEARY, Timothy	1827	12-351	Deborah	1810	9- 79
OLEPHANT, Jane	1828	13-129	Elizabeth	1783	3-523
OLER, George	1828	13- 96	Ephraim	1784	3-566
John	1848	22-372	Hannah	1819	10-561
Margaret	1850	23-348	Henry	1764	2-185
Peter	1840	18-155	Henry	1813	9-389
Philip	1826	12-245	John	1765	3- 8
OLIVER, John	1791	5- 22	John	1779	3-384
John	1823	11-583	John	1847	23-125
Robert	1835	15-213	John C.	1810	8-471
Thomas	1849	23-144	John C.	1813	9-321
OLMSTEAD, Alexander H.	1846	21-246	Joshua	1843	19-427
OLTON, John	1709	1- 34	Levi	1846	21- 61
O'NEAL, Jeremiah	1815	10- 57	Nicholas	1841	18-464
Thomas	1836	16-103	Richard	1786	4-180 & 184
O'NEILL, Charles	1832	14-258	Richard	1806	8- 34
ONION, Beale H.	1833	14-286	Ruth	1827	12-395
Eliza	1834	14-490	Ruth	1835	15-344
Elizabeth	1839	17-298	Samuel	1775	3-299
Stephen	1754	2- 62	Samuel	1803	7-197
Thomas B.	1812	9-286	Samuel	1828	13-115
ORFFER, Dinah	1844	20-206	Susannah	1797	6- 70
O'ROURK, Patrick	1806	8-116	Stephen H.	1821	11-247
ORRICK, James	1821	11-250	Thomas	1822	11-447
John	1811	9-110	Urath	1793	5- 70
John C.	1805	7-359	William	1825	12-157
Sarah	1838	17- 1	OYSTON, Benjamin	1832	14-121
William	1833	14-312	Henry	1782	3-479
ORSLER, Edward	1795	5-244	John	1803	7-134
John	1844	20-180	Laurence	1800	6-241
OSBORN, Daniel	1790	4-501	William	1802	6-532
James	1793	5-123 & 124	OZBORN, Benjamin	1760	2-277

PACA, Aquila	1721	1-494	PARRISH, Elizabeth	1748	1-445
Aquila	1743	2- 6	John	1746	1-371
John, Jr., .	1757	2-223	John	1785	4- 87
Martha	1746	1-358	Richard	1820	11-178
Rachel	1746	1-365	William	1728	1-220
PACKER, Aaron	1802	7- 14	PARROTT, Ann E.	1840	18- 49
PAGE, Bartholomew	1805	7-418	David	1840	17-471
Daniel	1828	13- 13'	PARRY, Ann	1848	22-135
PAICE, James B.	1848	22-161	Seneca	1845	21- 22
PAILLOTTET, Margaret	1817	10-348	Thomas	1838	16-469
PAINE, Elizabeth	1846	21-209	PARSONS, Daniel, Jr.	1821	11-222
Mary	1848	22-185	Mary	1848	22-331
Philip	1846	21-238	Thomas	1849	23-277
PALMER, Benjamin	1848	22-387	PATRTRIDGE, Daubeney B.	1762	3-119
John	1812	9-288	Jane		2-339
Thomas	1841	18-295	John	1831	14- 69
PANNELL, Edward	1835	15-279	Joseph G.	1831	14- 43
Edward, Jr.	1833	14-362	Letitia	1811	9-117
John	1799	6-156	William	1796	5-351
PARKER, Benjamin	1829	13-250	William	1811	9-140
Esther	1808	8-363	PASCAL, Peter	1849	23-141
Henry	1806	8- 82	PASCAULT, Mary	1831	13-503
John	1807	8-239	PATAT, John	1798	6-141
Margaret	1845	20-234	PATTEN, George	1778	3-372
Milla	1823	11-565	James	1831	14- 74
Peter	1818	10-534	PATTERSON, Abigail L.	1842	19-162
Quinton	1675	1-10	Ann	1828	13- 87
Robert	1815	10- 58	David	1834	15- 99
Susan	1845	22-413	Edward	1808	8-337
Thomas	1817	10-332	James	1806	8- 59
PARKIN, Thomas	1797	6- 8	Joseph	1831	14- 17
PARKS, Abraham	1845	20-281	Robert	1765	3- 10
Aquila	1801	6-399	Robert	1822	11-475
David	1814	9-498	William	1835	15-254
Elisha	1787	4-224	William	1846	21- 40
Frederick	1828	13- 73	William, Jr.	1808	8-360
John	1788	4-314	PAULL, William	1837	16-408
John	1812	9-264	PAULY, Christian	1786	4-119
John S.	1824	12- 15	Daniel	1808	8-356
Keziah	1782	3-467	PAWSON, Matthew	1804	7-303
Margaret	1813	9-327	PAXON, Samuel	1803	7-181
Mary	1842	19-114	PAYNE, Albert H.	1839	17-375
Nathan	1825	12-127	Elizabeth	1783	3-525
Ruth	1849	23-131	Elizabeth	1787	4-257
William	1823	11-591	William	1769	3- 61
PARLET, Hannah	1829	13-215	PAYSON, Henry	1845	21- 29
William	1780	3-411	PEACHIM, Elizabeth B.	1829	13-266
PARRISH, David	1813	9-297	PEACOCK, George	1836	16- 5
Edward	1773	3-240	Jacob	1713	1-122
Edward	1835	15-379			

PEACOCK, Jane	1713	1-123		PERIGO, Joseph	1800	6-319
PEALE, Elizabeth	1786	4-150		Mary	1849	23- 93
St. George	1776	3-362		Moses	1833	14-365
PEARCE, Druscilla	1840	18-119		PERINE, Margaret	1829	13-212
Ezra	1829	13-282		Margaret	1843	19-335
John	1820	11-102		Simon	1823	11-578
Joseph	1835	15-246		Temperance	1843	19-470
Nathan	1841	18-354		William	1768	3- 95
Thomas	1846	21-299		William	1826	12-267
William	1835	15-389		PERKEPEAL, Andrew	1773	3-251
PEARSE, William W.	1822	11-341		PERKINS, Benjamin	1799	6-163
PEARSON, Henry	1769	3-134		Elisha	1840	18- 1
PECK, John S.	1818	10-459		Elizabeth F.	1850	23-342
PECKETT, William	1710	1- 30		PERLEY, Ebenezer	1820	11-156
PEDDICOART, Benedict	1793	5-110		PERRY, Alexander	1781	3-441
William	1776	3-320		Jeremiah	1843	19-237
William	1779	3-374		Nicholas	1802	7-104
PEDUZZI, Peter	1827	12-341		PERRYMAN, Roger	1749	1-463
PEERCE, Edward	1823	11-576		PESTOW, Robert L.	1794	5-175
PEIN, Frederick	1824	11-638		PETERKIN, George W.	1837	16-417
Philipena	1850	23-448		PETERS, Anna	1843	19-418
PEINEMANN, Henry L. G.	1850	23-360		Elizabeth	1797	5-478
PEIRPOINT, Jabez	1721	1-513		Elizabeth	1837	16-291
PEMBERTON, Henry	1812	9-227		George	1850	23-377
Joshua	1828	13- 53		Henry	1838	16-447
Margaret	1815	10- 42		Jacob	1828	13- 66
PENDERGAST, Patrick	1817	10-365		John	1805	8- 8
PENN, Caleb	1811	9-197		John	1830	13-459
Caroline	1818	10-530		Rebecca	1837	16-369
John	1791	4-530		Richard	1848	22-416
Joshua	1843	19-207		William	1815	10- 72
Nathan	1803	7-250		PETRI, Conrad	1850	23-457
Miriam	1831	13-496		PETTIGREW, Ebenezer	1849	23- 62
William	1846	21-237		PEVERILLE, Joseph	1798	6-134
PENNACK, Martha	1845	20-469		PEYTON, Ylverton T.	1831	14- 24
PENNEBACKER, William	1814	9-421		PHILIPS, Ephraim	1813	9-326
PENNINGTON, James	1678	1- 66		Francis	1771	3-197
Josias	1810	9- 60		Henry	1786	4-155
Henry P.	1825	12-154		Mary	1792	5- 43
Mary	1842	19- 63		Zachariah	1822	11-495
Mary Wm.	1837	16-230		PHILLIPS, Anthony	1695	1-180
PENRICE, John	1714	1-125		Eliza	1837	16-207
Thomas	1820	11-157		James	1689	1-250
PERCIVAL, Thomas F.	1811	9-112		James	1720	1-161
PERDUE, Walter	1828	13-134		James	1849	23-133
PEREGOY, Henry	1802	7- 5		John	1765	3- 23
John	1838	17-133		John	1827	13- 6
PERIGO, James	1817	10-293		John T.	1830	13-453
James	1840	18-129		Juliann	1834	14-467
John	1796	5-360		Lemuel	1831	14- 40

INDEX OF BALTIMORE COUNTY WILLS

PHILLIPS, Samuel	1829	13-303	POLLITT, Sarah R.	1846	21-136'
Sophia	1822	11-419	PONS, Anthony	1797	5-477
Susan A.	1832	14-164	PONTANY, Edward	1778	3-368
Thomas	1847	22- 69	POOL, Elizabeth	1833	14-361
Thomas	1808	8-333	POOR, Samuel	1821	11-330
William	1788	4-291	POPPLEIN, Andrew	1848	22-209
PHIPPS, Nathaniel	1791	5- 21	Nicholas	1837	16-421
PICKHAVER, Jonathan	1809	8-428	PORTER, Francis	1709	1- 28
PICKETT, Jeremiah	1797	5-496	James	1799	6-154
PIECAZAM, Robert	1801	6-432	John, Jr.	1842	18-484
PIERCE, Edward	1823	11-576	Michael	1824	12- 72
George C.	1829	13-207	Ralph	1822	11-500
PIERPOINT, Benedict	1836	16-158	Richard	1789	4-363
Charles	1785	4- 33	Robert	1810	8-493
Joseph	1821	11-210	William	1835	15-299
PILSCH, Anton	1844	19-482	William A.	1843	19-310
PINAULT, Rene	1805	7-444	PORTEUS, Robert	1786	4-170
PINDELL, John	1789	4-374	POTEE, Peter	1833	14-365
John	1817	10-302	POTEE. See also PUTTEE.		
Thomas	1793	5-120	POTEET, Jesse	1848	22-151
PINKNEY, Ninian	1826	12-220	POTET, John	1809	8-445
William E.	1825	12- 86	POVIER, Peter	1796	5-374
PIPER, James	1803	7- 99	POUDER, Mary M.	1846	21-141
William	1785	4- 56	POULTNEY, Thomas	1829	13-157
PISTON, John C.	1844	20- 16	POWELL, Benjamin	1788	4-321
PITT, Thomas	1820	11- 95	Isaac	1841	18-217
William	1849	23- 54	John	1818	10-502
PITTS, John	1785	4- 80	Mary	1806	8- 44
Lewis	1829	13-263	Patrick B.	1816	10-214
PLAT, James	1801	6-434	POWER, James	1825	12-139
PLATT, Ann	1809	8-378	John	1840	18- 51
PLOWMAN, Jonathan	1776	3-318	Michael	1845	20-347
Jonathan	1795	5-333	PRACHT, John	1846	21-260
Rebecca	1778	3-374	PRADERE, John	1813	9-334
POE, Elizabeth	1838	17- 38	PRATT, Charles M.	1842	19-111
George	1823	11-594	Henry	1838	17- 81
POCOCK, Daniel	1784	3-572	PRATTON, Caroline F.	1804	7-277
James	1806	8- 50	PRENDERGAST, Guy Lenox	1850	23-332
John	1791	4-551	PRENDERVILLE, Garret	1813	9-301
Susannah	1785	4- 34	PRENTICE, Alexander	1842	19- 30
Thomas	1844	20-185	PRESBURY, George G., Jr.		
POGUE, Elizabeth	1847	21-324		1810	9- 54
POILARD, John	1761	2-354	Geo. Gouldsmith	1822	11-389
POLAND, Adam	1831	14- 23	James	1746	1-362
POLEY, Jacob	1800	6-251	Mary Matilda	1821	11-303
POLK, Gillis R. M. W.	1804	7-299	Priscilla	1827	12-353
James	1818	10-475	PRESS, Henry	1786	4-131
Robert	1777	3-347	PRESSMAN, Thomas	1835	15-412
POLLARD, George	1834	15-196	PRESTMAN, Geo.	1819	11- 35
John	1761	2-354	PRESTON, Daniel	1772	3-211

PRESTON, James	1729	2-191
James, Jr.	1762	2 158
James	1766	3- 48
Thomas	1710	1-260
William	1796	5-465
William	1828	13-145
PRETLOVE, Sarah	1848	22-388
PREVETORY, Elizabeth	1838	17- 18
PRICHARD, Samuel	1774	3-297
PRICE, Abraham H.	1833	14-313
Absolom	1781	3-435
Beal	1846	21- 99
Benj.	1814	9-444
Daniel	1806	8- 45
Daniel	1846	21-235
		& 357
Howell	1841	18-319
Isabella	1836	16- 65
James	1807	8-197
James	1814	9-442
James B.	1848	22-161
John	1782	3-496
John	1789	4-422
John	1790	4-502
John	1809	8-403
John	1825	12-133
Joshua	1802	6-544
Joshua	1841	18-341
Kitturah	1829	13-207
Leah	1835	15-413
Martha	1835	15-292
Mary	1833	14-310
Milley	n. d.	9-453
Millison	1787	4-243
Mordecai	1796	5-379
Mordecai	1807	8-235
Nehemiah	1818	10-503
Nicodemus	1849	23- 78
Samuel	1800	6-302
Samuel	1825	12-130
Samuel	1844	20-175
Sophia	1824	12- 61
Stephen	1809	8-438
Thomas	1741	1-390
Thomas, Sr.	1844	20- 44
Thomas, Sr.	1847	22- 38
William	1819	11- 7
William	1831	14- 80
William W.	1805	7-448
Zachariah	1807	8-271

PRIESTLEY, Edward	1837	16-224
PRIMAS, James	1819	11- 89
PRIMAVESI, Francis	1809	8-409
PRINCE, Caesar	1676	1-112
John	1845	20-315
PRITCHARD, Joseph	1733	2-291
Margaret	1739	1-318
Obadiah	1727	1-240
PROCTOR, Isaiah P.	1807	8-246
John	1791	4-515
PROUT, Robert	1827	12-410*
William B.	1837	16-232*
PROSSER, Isaac	1827	12-354
PROUT, Richard	1814	9-444*
PUE, Arthur	1847	22- 79
Mary	1807	8-259
Mary	1833	14-379
Rebecca	1835	15-284
PULLEN, Randall	1850	23-315
PUMPHREY, Francis	1825	12-103
Walter	1720	1-161
PURCELL, Henry	1800	6-311
PURNELL, Isaac	1813	9-360
PURVIANCE, Robert	1806	8-111
PUTSON, Martin	1818	10-452
PUTTEE, Peter	1740	1-327
Rebecca	1758	2- 80
Puttee. See also Potee.		
PYCRAFT, Thomas	1767	3- 5
PYKE, Abraham	1844	20- 34
QUARLES, John	1846	21-317
QUARY, Sarah	1844	20- 14
QUAY, Thomas	1828	13- 44
QUEEN, George	1810	9- 59
QUICKLEY, Caesar	1846	21- 85
QUIGLEY, James	1815	10- 53
QUINLAN, James	1825	12- 90
QUINN, Edward	1834	14-466
Simon	1795	5-231
QUITMAN, Henry S.	1848	22-149
RAAB, Adam G.	1813	9-374
Dietrick	1823	11-577
Lena	1847	21-429
RABORG, Rebecca	1833	14-287
RABURG, Geo. W.	1817	10-273

RADDAD, Matthew	1797	6- 27		REAVES, William	1764	2-174
RADISH, Thomas	1766	3- 36		RECIUD, Clement	1824	12- 79
RAHM, Jacob	1778	3-360		REED, Elizabeth	1846	21-124
RAILLY, William	1840	18- 42		Emanuel	1802	7- 82
RAITT, John	1833	14-311		John	1839	17-259
RALPH, George	1813	9-327		John Denel	1791	5- 4
RALSTON, Gwynn?	1760	2-278		Mary	1813	9-337
RAMSAY, Charlotte	1838	16-521		Nancy	1849	23-235
		& 523		Nelson	1840	18-123
Thomas	1817	10-391		REES, Solomon	1752	2- 45
RAMSEY, John	1803	7=241		REESE, Adam	1800	6-321
Nathaniel	1817	10-375		Ann	1827	12-402
RANDALL, Bale	1822	11-407		George	1803	7-180
Charlotte	1841	18-291		George Daniel	1848	22-197
Christopher	1735	2-206		REEVES, Anthony	1802	7- 78
Deborah	1839	17-373		REHINE, Zalma	1843	19-359
Elisha	1846	21-129		REID, James	1850	23-458
Hannah	1727	1-237		REIDASIL, Mary	1848	22-257
Isaac	1844	20-169		REIGART, Susanna	1843	19-393
John C.	1817	10-395		REILLY, Mary	1834	15- 31
Larkin W.	1828	13-119		Michael	1846	21-272
Richard	1795	5-241		Peter	1835	15-324
Thomas	1812	9-221		Philip	1839	17-384
RANKIN, Christopher	1826	12-244		REIMAN, Samuel	1841	18-176
RANTZ, Susanna	1773	3-263		REINAGLE, Alexander	1809	8-446
RAPHEL, Stephen	1811	9-311		REINHART, David	1842	19-194
RAPP, Hannah	1831	14- 75		REINICKER, Conrad	1810	8-499
RATLOFF, William	1849	23-227		George	1838	17- 21
RATREN, Diedrich	1826	12-269		John	1815	10- 61
alias Richard Ratren.				REISTER, Eve	1839	17-369
RATRIE, Jane	1808	8-358		Henry	1830	13-386
RATTENBURY, John	1746	1-372		John	1804	7-355
RAVEN, Ann	1833	14-365		John	1841	18-216
Isaac	1826	12-228		Peter	1845	20-448
Luke	1761	2-349		REITER, William Lewis		
Luke	1802	6-489		Christian	1822	11-470
Luke	1805	8- 19		RENAUD, Margaret	1818	10-407
Sarah	1795	5-296		RENCHER, Richard M.	1845	20-399
Thomas L.	1834	15- 42		RENELIS, John W.	1818	10-542
RAVIS, Thomas	1827	12-333		RENNER, John	1821	11-287
RAWLING, Joseph	1795	5-251		RENSHAW, John	1751	3-414
RAWLINGS, Elizabeth	1840	17-469		Thomas	1748	1-416
John	1722/3	1-222		REPLE, Nicholas	1818	10-518
William	1812	9-259		REPOLD, Metta	1826	12-249
RAYHICE, Joseph	1820	11-161		REPPERT, Jacob	1837	16-371
RAYMOND, Peter G.	1832	14-125		Lewis	1822	11-343
RAYNAUD, Peter G.	1832	14-127		RESCANIERE, Peter	1831	14- 11
REA, George	1806	8- 77		RESIDE, Edward	1827	12-338
READ, William George	1846	21-147		William	1839	17-394
Reaston. See Riston.				RETECER, Jacob	1784	3-570

RINGGOLD, Jacob	1816	10-136		ROBINSON, Henry	1849	23- 17
Martha	1812	9-284		James	1695	1- 63
Samuel	1846	21-255		Joseph	1845	30-374
RIPPLE, Margaret	1848	22-458		Margaret	1850	23-469
RISCHSTEIN, George	1838	17- 40		Matilda	1845	20-379
RISTEAU, Abraham	1783	3-519		Rachel	1823	11-588
Catherine	1762	2-148		Richard	1770	3-169
Charles W.	1842	19- 37		Robert	1735,	1-283
George, Jr.	1789	4-356		Samuel	1802	7- 87
George	1792	5- 42		Samuel, Jr.	1829	13-325
Isaac	1764	2-159		Sophia	1790	4-402
John	1760	2-273		William	1844	20- 88
Thomas	1796	5-452				& 118
RISTER, John	1814	9-428		ROCHE, John	1817	10-346
RISTON, Edward	1749	1-471		ROCKHOLD, Asel	1773	3-244
RITSCHHUT, John	1832	14-134		Charles	1741	1-340
RITTER, Anthony	1779	3-386		Edmund	1847	21-396
Thomas	1845	20-463		or Edward.		
ROACH, John	1765	3- 19		Jacob	1827	12-340
Jane	1849	23- 56		Jacob	1829	13-221
John	1830	13-388		Mary	1704	1- 14
ROADS, Christopher	1808	8-361		Mary	1830	13-466
ROBARDS, John	1779	3-383		RODE, Morik	1800	6-276
ROBB, George	1829	13-214		ROESNER, Johanna	1822	11-486
Capt. John	1805	7-435		ROGERS, Ann	1841	18-247
ROBERIT, Francis D. M. I.				Augustus	1796	5-424
	1799	6-198		Catherine	1799	6-232
ROBERT, Saladine V.	1810	9- 32		Charles	1806	8- 21
ROBERTS, George, Sr.	1797	6- 41		Edward	1824	12- 66
George	1827	13- 12		Elizabeth	1828	13-118
John	1728	2-189				& 119
John	1779	3-383		Henry C.	1825	12-200
Jonathan	1841	18-235		John H.	1823	11-547
Mareen	1754	2- 57		Nicholas	1720	1-151
Peter	1823	11-517		Nicholas	1758	2- 64
Thomas	1709	1- 20		Nicholas	1822	11-354
ROBERTSON, Charles	1834	15-135		Philip	1836	16-112
Robert	1748	1-276		Samuel R.	1805	7-405
Sarah	1748	1-450		Sarah	1791	5- 78
ROBINSON, Alexander	1845	20-417		Sarah	1808	8-296
		& 495		Thomas	1820	11-204
Archibald	1797	6- 17		William	1761	2-319
Catherine	1842	19-179		William	1784	4- 17
Charles	1772	3-233		William S.	1843	19-212
Charles	1835	15-373		ROHR, Andrew	1825	12-116
Dorcas	1842	19- 54		ROHRER, John	1767	3- 72
Dorsey	1815	9-519		ROLLES, Jacob. See Rowles, Jacob.		
Eve	1842	19-180		ROLLINGS, Richard	1783	3-537
George	1784	3-575		ROLLINS, Edward	1841	18-165
George	1784	4-109		William	1824	12- 4

ROLLO, Archibald	1747	1 -401
ROMYN, John H.	1839	17-206
ROOKER, Samuel	1829	13-165
ROOT, William	1850	23-415
ROSE, Mary	1819	10-595
ROSMAN, Edward. See Bosman, Edward.		
ROSS, Charles M.	1849	23-222
David	1762	2-155
Elizabeth	1840	17-482
Elizabeth	1841	18-375
		& 376
James	1808	8-339
John	1782	3-484
John	1809	8-389
Joseph	1839	17-191
Mary	1819	10-595
Reuben	1830	13-407
Sarah A.	1824	11-652
William	1820	11-151
ROUNDLEY, Margaret	1799	6-230
ROURK, Patrick O.	1806	8-116
ROUSE, James	1788	4-301
ROWLAND, Thomas	1783	3-540
ROWLES, Anna Maria	1812	9-278
David	1780	3-408
Jacob	1768	3- 84
Jacob	1818	10-538
Rezin	1849	23-106
William	1750	2- 31
William	1773	3-237
ROWLET, Mary	1794	5-211
ROY, John	1820	11-183
ROYCROFT, John	1675	1-199
ROYSTON, John	1798	6-104
Ruth	1839	17-250
Sarah	1804	7-274
William	1847	22- 75
ROZER, John	1799	6-164
RUCKLE, George	1839	17-208
Paul	1848	22-384
RUDDACH, Jane	1831	14- 99
Joseph	1832	14-170
RUDDEROW, Spicer	1839	17-332
RUDEN, Jacques	1806	8-225
RUDENSTEIN, John M.	1834	15- 85
RUFF, Daniel	1749	1-466
Richard	1733	2-289
Sarah	1747	1-398
Sarah	1822	11-490
RUHL, Peter	1848	22-187

RUHLE, George	1815	10- 13
RUHLING, Charles	1847	21-430
RUL, Peter	1815	10- 34
RULE, Jacob	1816	10-149
RUMSEY, Charles Henry	1829	13-210
Henrietta	1838	17-122
Mary	1837	16-304
RUP, Michael	1816	10-151
RUPERT, John	1805	7-447
RUSH, John	1796	5-525
Robert	1813	9-388
RUSSELL, Archibald	1820	11-144
Elizabeth	1845	20-286
George	1816	10-237
Henry	1846	21- 68
Rebecca	1840	18-107
Richard	1821	11-322
William	1849	23- 78
RUST, Magdalena	1841	18-314
RUTH, Jehu	1805	7-426
or John.		
RUTLEDGE, Abraham	1807	8-263
Ephraim	1800	6-314
John	1773	3-270
John	1841	18-194
Thomas	1832	14-123
RUTTER, Garrett	1664	1- 64
John	1806	8- 61
Mary	1779	3-388
Richard	1757	2-238
Richard	1838	17- 31
Solomon	1821	11-296
Thomas	1746	1-353
RYAN, Dennis	1786	4-138
RYLAND, Nicholas	1825	12-165
SABEL, Leonard	1795	5-260
SADLER, Thomas	1801	6-394
ST. CLAIR, Williamina	1825	12-188
See also Sinclair, Sinklar.		
ST. John	1835	15-365
SALENAVE, Bernard	1816	10-106
James	1837	16-316
SALISBURY, Levi	1813	9-300
SALMON, George	1807	8-237
John	1826	12-325
John	1829	13-315
SALTER, Cornelius	1801	6-452
		& 454

SAMPSON, Isaac	1836	16- 89
Richard	1714	1-121
SANDELL, Edward	1822	11-406
SANDERS, Benedict Joseph	1845	20-227 & 231
Blanche	1824	11-625
Elizabeth	1787	4-237
Zachariah	1850	23-218
SANDERSON, Margaret	n. d.	4- 71
Margaret	1808	8-282
Margaret	1816	10-224
Michael	1823	11-506
SANDOZ, John	1789	4-376
SANDS, Francis	1770	3-167
John	1829	13-176
SANFORD, Samuel	1797	6- 15
SANKEY, Samuel Giles	1841	18-229
SANKS, John	1827	12-373
Mary	1831	13-475
SANNER, Elizabeth	1817	10-349
John	1835	15-251
Jonathan B.	1847	21-458
SANTZ, Peter	1807	8-184
SARGENTS, Samuel	1824	12- 33
SAUBLE, Michael	1827	12-352
SAUERWEIN, Peter	1836	16-116
SAUL, Isabella	1803	7-214
SAUNDERS, Charles	1811	9-214
Edward	1770	3-173
SAUTER, Christian	1850	23-463
SAVAGE, Ann	1843	19-312
David	1825	12-174
Dennis	1814	9-467
Patrick	1812	9-233
William	1785	4- 68
SAVORY, Rosanna	1843	19-223
William	1839	17-361
SCARBOROUGH, Abraham	1838	16-434
SCARF, Henry	1845	20-242
William	1806	8- 77
SCARFF, Sarah	1782	3-462
SCARLETT, Boitha	1790	4-508
SCHAEFFER, Baltzer	1838	17- 44
Benjamin	1831	14- 67
SCHARFF, William	1840	18- 20
SCHEDDLEMEYER, Mary	1769	3-133
SCHEITHAUER, Henry	1838	16-476
SCHISS, Jacob	1848	22-461
SCHLEICH, John or Schleigh.	1802	7-118
SCHMACKPEPER, John R.	1823	11-602

SCHNAUBER, George	1815	10- 61
SCHNEIDER, Theobald	1784	4- 18
SCHOLTZ, Sam'l Godlieb	1786	4-178
SCHORR, Michael	1834	15-207
SCHREIBER, Mary F.	1813	9-306
Rev. Peters	1845	20-468
SCHROEDER, Edward	1847	21-361
Mary	1840	17-462
SCHULTE, Philip	1821	11-298
SCHULTZE, Christopher	1805	7-453
J. E. C.	1818	10-419
John H.	1848	22-264
SCHUMAKER, Jonathan	1811	9- 90
SCHWARTZ, Frederick	1816	10-115
SCHWARTZE, August P.	1850	23-419
Henry	1850	23-274
SCHWARTZMAN, Joseph	1846	21- 55
SCHWARZAUER, Daniel	1847	22- 56
SCHWATKA, August	1846	21- 64
SCHWEITZER, Jacob	1832	14-156
SCLATTER, Elizabeth	1848	22-193
SCOGGINS, Amy	1820	11-122
SCORCE, John	1768	3- 94
William	1781	3-430
SCOTT, Abraham	1803	7-176
Ann, Sr.	1834	14-432
Aquila	1760	2-274
Daniel	1745	2-212
Daniel	1752	2- 40
Elizabeth	1758	2- 66
Elizabeth	1760	2- 277
George	1837	16-280
Henry	1818	10-405
Jacob	1767	3- 77
James	1762	2-151 & 159
Jesse	1843	19-468
Jesse	1849	23-123
John	1830	13-431
John	1846	21-250 & 265
John	1850	23-345
John Henry	1837	16-223
Joseph	1802	6-501
Louisa	1818	10-486
Rossiter	1830	13-409
Samuel	1807	8-157
Thomas	1817	10-383
SCUTT, John	1703	1- 16
SEABROOK, Eliza S.	1834	15- 49
SEALL, William	1767	3- 70

SEARS. Lucretia	1845	20-342		SHARE, Joseph	1849	23-112
See also pp. 444 and 449				SHARP, Ann	1845	20-249
Sarah	1843	19-465		John	1790	4-411
SEATON, James	1783	3-521		Susanna	1809	8-382
SEAVEY, William	1831	14- 5		SHAULE, Joseph	1785	4- 86
SEDDON, James	1825	12- 94		SHAVER, Abraham	1846	21-112
		& 131		Christian	1785	4- 78
James	1850	23-355		John Adam	1793	5-124
John	1824	12- 55		SHAW, Ann	1844	20- 23
Margaret	1844	20-222		Archibald	1845	20-380
		& 226		Christopher	1739	1-320
Sarah	1832	14-116		Christopher	1747	1-404
Zachariah	1827	12-343		Daniel	1807	8-187
SEDERBERG, Truls	1841	18-272		George	1826	12-288
SEEBACH, Wilhelmina	1834	14-434		John	1749	1-472
SEEDERS, Henry	1809	8-421		John	1808	8-286
SEEKAMP, Albert	1840	18- 55		Dr. John, Jr.	1809	8-405
SEESNAP, Adam	1831	14- 17		Joshua	1838	17-146
SEGAN, Pero	1834	15- 46		Nancy	1824	12- 50
SEGUIN, Francis	1811	9-120		Robert	1813	9-307
SEIXAS, Benj.	1847	21-370		Samuel	1823	11-514
SELBY, Philip	1786	4-135		Samuel	1844	19-497
SELLMAN, Elizabeth	1848	22-319		Sarah	1802	7-130
George Mayo	1814	9-462		Thomas	1806	8- 48
Johnzee	1818	10-461		Thomas	1829	13-332
Mary	1825	12-169		Thomas Knightsmith	1794	5-213
Rachel	1823	11-521				& 219
SELTZER, Adam	1849	23-288		William Checkley	1848	22-407
Mary	1849	23- 28		William G.	1834	14-472
SERJEANT, John	1748	1-441		SHAWN, Nicholas	1810	6-457
SETTLER, Mathias, Sr.	1787	4-261		SHEA, Thomas	1767	3- 74
SETTON, James	1783	3-521		SHEAN, Daniel	1825	12-212
SEWALL, Comfort	1785	4-101		SHEARMILLER, Godlip	1781	3-427
SEWELL, Elizabeth	1820	11-200		SHEEAN, William	1785	4-105
John	1848	22-336		SHELMERDINE, John	1778	3-357
SEXTON, Charles	1827	12-433		SHEPHERD, Rowland	1731	1-269
SHADE, John	1824	12- 42		Temperance	1802	7- 97
SHAFER, Jacob	1802	7- 33		SHEPPARD, James	1767	3- 76
SHAFFER, Benj.	1832	14-113		John	1800	6-281
Frederick	1844	20- 24		SHEREDINE, Daniel	1749	1-472
Jacob	1800	6-249		Thomas	1769	3-164
John	1828	13- 50		SHERLOCK, Louisa	1818	10-516
SHALLCROSS, Thomas	1805	7-434		SHERMAN, Conrad	1824	11-629
SHAMBURG, Henry	1844	20-155		SHERRINGTON, William	1834	15-200
SHAMMOND, Mary Rose	1798	6- 77		SHERWOOD, Mary	1827	13- 9
SHANKLIN, Robert	1838	16-467		SHIELDS, Jane	1825	12-115
SHANLEY, Godfrey	1809	8-388		Thomas	1846	21-101
Dr. Jeffrey Dillon	1809	8-388		SHILLING, Michael	1798	6- 99
John	1843	19-431		SHIPLEY, Absalom	1809	8-359
SHANNON, Patrick	1825	12-137		Adam	1818	10-546

SHIPLEY, Benj.	1812	9-219		SIMPSON, Jonathan	1786	4-167
Charles	1815	10- 67		Richard	1711	1- 88
Peter	1782	3-472		SIMS, Mary	1761	2-335
Peter	1821	11-226		SINCLAIR, Aaron	1812	9-210
Peter	1823	11-570		Edward	1779	3-391
Richard	1725	1-205		William	1830	13-469
Robert, of Adam	1822	14-124		William W.	1828	13- 76
Samuel	1780	3-396		SINCLAR, Mary	1771	3-181
SHOCK, Hannah	1824	12- 69				& 182
SHOEMAKER, George	1848	22-215		See also St. Clair, Sinklar.		
SHOOK, Geo.	1820	11-144		SINDAL, Samuel	1800	6-266
SHORB, Andrew	1844	20-125		SINDALL, David	1794	5-154
SHORR, Michael	1834	15-207		Elizabeth	1817	10-306
SHORT, Nathan	1810	9- 74		Jacob	1779	3-386
SHOTT, Jacob, Jr.	1834	15-193		Philip	1738	1-302
SHOWERS, John	1810	8-485		Philip	1816	10-240
SHRANK, John	1784	4- 13		William	1828	13- 88
SHRECK, George W.	1843	19- 466		SINGERY, Christian	1817	10-394
SHRIVER, John	1805	7-425		SINKLAIR, Nathan	1777	3-365
Mary	1813	9-306		SINKLER, William	1795	5-273
SHROYER, George	1775	3-308		See also St. Clair, Sinclair.		
SHRYER, Lewis	1805	8- 20		SINNARD, John	1821	11-208
SHRYOCK, John	1836	16- 53		SISCO, Charles	1846	21-125
SHUGERS, Edward	1822	11-496		SITLEMEYER, Bastian	1760	2- 85
SHULTE, John	1820	11-134		SITLER, Abraham	1800	6-243
Philip	1821	11-298		Barbara	1814	9-473
SHULTZ, Christopher	1805	7-453		Elizabeth	1850	23-480
J. E. C.	1818	10-419		SITTLER, Mathias	1787	4-261
John Grandadans	1829	13-166		SKELTON, Israel	1706	1- 67
John H.	1848	22-264		SKIFF, Joseph	1835	15-372
SHUTE, John	1763	3- 1		SKILLMAN, Hannah	1845	20-454
SICKLEMORE, Sutton	1765	3- 21		SKINNER, John	1806	8- 52
SIDES, Aaron	1816	10-186		SKIPHART, Mary	1785	4- 90
SIEGEMAN, Henry	1846	21- 53		SLADE, Abraham	1847	22- 51
SIEMEN, Paul	1832	14-186		Delilah	1846	21-191
SIEMER, John	1827	12-356		Elizabeth	1838	17-143
SIEMERS, Gerhard	1844	20-132		Thomas	1838	17-139
SILVERTHORN, Stephen	1825	12-114		William	1785	4- 48
SIMKINS, Eli	1817	10-321		SLEIGER, Philip L.	1798	6- 82
John	1739	1-300		SLAGER, Philip L.	1798	6- 82
SIMLER, George	1823	11-587		SLATER, Henry	1754	2-271
SIMMONS, Abraham	1815	10- 17		SLEE, Elizabeth	1818	10-456
Charles	1788	1-298		Joseph	1814	9-509
Priscilla	1832	14-217		Joseph	1830	13-393
Samuel	1832	14-227		SLEEPER, Jacob	1819	11- 14
William	1810	9- 73		SLEMAKER, James	1750	2- 30
SIMES, James	1805	8- 11		SLEUFF, Jacob	1782	3-477
SIMONDS, Joseph	1691	1-111		SLIGH, Thomas	1774	3-293
SIMONS, John	1815	10- 42		SLOAN, John	1847	21-432
SIMPSON, Elizabeth	1832	14-263		Thomas	1833	14-302

SMALL, Michael	1826	12-221	SMITH, Joseph	1817	10-273
William F.	1832	14-183	Laken	1846	21- 60
SMART, David	1822	11-463	Larkin H.	1844	20-111
SMITH, Adam	1826	12-255	Leonard	1791	5- 1
Andrew	1811	9-126	Margaret	1843	19-202.
Andrew	1811	9-148	Margaret	1850	23-465
Arnold	1813	9-393	Mary	1823	11-622
Casper	1818	10-526	Mary	1826	12-222
Conrad	1777	3-332	Mary	1831	13-497
David	1805	7-423	Mary	1843	19-384
David	1810	9- 58	Mary Blakely	1822	11-483
Deborah	1767	3- 73	Nicholas	1804	7-278
Edward	1730	1-242	Polly	1825	12-129
Edward	1846	21-117	Priscilla	1839	17-236
		& 497	Rachel	1849	23-196
Elihu	1849	23-243	Ralph	1771	3-193
Elizabeth	1770	3-175	Ralph	1827	12-377
Elizabeth	1816	10-222	Richard	1797	6- 13
Elizabeth	1818	10-485	Richard C.	1818	10-430
Elizabeth	1844	19-487	Robert	1721	2- 2
Emanuel	1704	1- 90	Robert	1820	11-182
Francis	1789	4-383	Robert	1843	19-214
Fra cis	1805	7-377	Roger	1833	14-317
Frederick M.	1839	17-391	Rowland	1784	4- 7
George	1704	1- 84	Salome	1850	23-411
George C.	1825	12-199	Samuel	1768	3-100
Hannah	1848	22-446	Samuel	1784	3-568
See also pp. 464, 470, 471.			Samuel	1822	11-413
Huldah	1773	3-248	Samuel	1839	17-286
Isaac	1849	23- 35	Samuel, Jr.	1850	23-417
Jacob	1818	10-479	Samuel R.	1831	14- 18
James	1800	6-339	Sarah	1830	13-449
James	1820	11-201	Sarah Heath	1820	11- 25
James	1831	14- 10	Susan	1847	22- 57
James	1834	15-141	Susannah	1824	12- 48
James	1841	18-283	Thomas	1717	1-146
James V.	1819	11- 42	Thomas	1831	13-498
Job	1832	14-118	Thomas	1838	16-497
John	1777	3-347	Thorowgood	1810	9- 33
John	1793	5-111	Walter	1770	3-217
John	1794	5-164	Wilhelmina	1825	12-172'
John	1847	21-470	William	1731	1-266
John	1847	21-485	William	1738	1-293
John, Sr.	1849	23-200	William	1743	1-347
John Addison	1776	3-322	William	1746	1-370
John E.	1841	18-412	William	1774	3-278
John L. M.	1844	20-136	William	1814	9-431
John M.	1815	10- 46	William	1823	11-579
John M.	1833	14-349	William J.	1811	9-112
Joseph	1770	3-168	William M.	1818	10-464

SMITHSON, Thomas	1732	1-259
SMULL, Conrad	1809	8-463
SMYSER, Peter	1834	15-124
SMYTH, Anthony	1846	21- 89
SMYTHE, Joseph	1818	10-438
SNECK, Henry	1831	14- 29
SNELSON, Abraham	1760	2-270
William	1741	1-391
SNIDER, Abraham	1799	6-184
Frederick	1841	18-368
Jacob	1779	3-390
Lewis	1811	9-124
Martin	1810	8-473
SNOWDEN, Eleanor	1812	9-260
John Baptist	1779	3-377
Mary	1810	8-475
SNYDER, Christian	1841	18-363
Hieronimus	1820	11-160
Mary M.	1841	18-298
Peter	1832	14-147
Valentine	1803	7-245
		& 262
William	1804	7-310
SOLLERS, Elisha	1809	8-454
Francis	1798	6- 87
James	1764	2-166
Mary	1773	3-242
Robert	1825	12-105
Sabrett	1760	2-267
Sabrett	1786	4-152
Thomas	1783	3-535
SOLOMON, Abigail	1812	9-216
Benj.	1844	20- 22
Isaac	1789	6- 76
Robert	1784	3-564
SOMERVELL, Ann	1842	19- 10
SOMERVILLE, Henry	1805	7-378
Henry	1837	16-345
William	1816	10-158
William C.	1826	12-270
SOPER, James	1811	9-180
SOUTHERLAND, St. Clair	1820	11-184
SPALDING, Mary Elizabeth	1848	22-203
William	1803	7-215
		& 221
SPAN, Samuel	1796	8- 64
SPARKS, Cassandra	1832	14-245
Dorcas	1843	19-434
Josiah	1846	21- 91
		& 93

SPARROW, Mary	1811	9-123
alias Helmo		
SPAVALD, James	1772	3-218
SPEAR, Anne	1836	16- 29
John	n. d.	5-377
William	1822	11-497
SPEARS, George	1807	8-165
SPECK, Henry	1800	6-242
SPENCE, Mary C.	1849	23-294
		& 316
Capt. Robert Traill		
	1826	12-303
SPENCER, Catherine	1844	20-190
William	1788	4-300
SPICER, John	1739	1-312
John	1788	4-287
Thomas	1748	1-434
Valentine	1799	6-236
SPICKNALL, John	1821	11-325
SPINDLER, Jacob	1800	6-294
John	1843	19-397
SPOTSWOOD, Daniel	1830	13-438
SPRIGG, Thomas	1833	14-335
SPRY, Johanna	1675	1- 6
SPURRIER, Green	1787	4-205
SQUIRE, Daniel	1804	7-289
STACKHOUSE, Charles	1806	8- 41
STACY, William	1798	6-102
STAETES, Catherine	1839	17-396
STAFFORD, Patrick	1814	9-503
		& 507
STALL, Barbara	1839	17-378
STAMMEN, Ulrich B.	1850	23-438
STANDAFORD, Mary	1849	23-216
STANDEFER, Samuel	1708	1- 20
STANDIFORD, John	1806	8- 76
John	1814	9-397
Skelton	1802	6-540
William	1776	3-330
STANLEY, Elizabeth	1810	9- 38
STANLY, Ann	1836	15-438
STANSBURY, Abraham	1811	9-174
Amelia	1824	12- 11
Caleb	1846	21-199
Charles	1806	8-125
Daniel	1803	7-256
Daniel	1813	9-336
Daniel	1817	10-336
Darius	1847	21-447
Deborah M.	1842	19-100

STANSBURY, Dixon, Sr.	1805	8- 10
Dixon	1832	14-135
Elizabeth	1799	6-228
Elizabeth	1837	16-426
Elizabeth	1847	22-101
Emanuel	1791	4-513
George	1789	4-358
Isaac	1816	10-117
Jacob	1812	9-212
James	1826	12-323
Jane	1759	2-304
John	1785	4-102
John E.	1841	18-236
Joseph	1798	6-150
Joseph W.	1810	9- 26
Josias	1825	12-131
Luke	1742	1-345
Mary Ann	1827	12-349
Rachel	1834	15- 47
Richard	1787	4-233
Richard	1791	5- 10
Richardson	1797	5-505
Richardson	1819	11- 71
Samuel	1783	3-539
Sarah	1806	8- 55
Sarah	1830	13-351
Solomon	1823	11-552
Thomas	1766	3- 46
Thomas, Sr.	1798	6-110
Thomas	1817	10-260
Tobias	1758	2- 68
Tobias	1764	2-167
Tobias, Sr.	1799	6-173
Tobias	1811	9- 88
Tobias	1850	23-319
William	1788	4-312
William	1821	11-283
William	1825	12-150
Zachariah	1822	11-491
STANYEA, Lawrence	1798	6-134
STAPEL, William	1824	12- 17
STAPLER, Joseph	1815	10- 63
STAPLETON, Joshua	1844	20-199
Mary	1812	9-280
STARCKE, Charles	1838	16-439
STARKEY, Joshua	1744	2- 19
STARR, Catherine	1839	17-381
Henry	1834	15-144
Isaac	1833	14-315
John	1829	13-163
STARR, Margaret	1848	22-258
Thomas	1842	19-153
William	1819	11- 23
STARTZMAN, Angellica	1849	23- 47
STAYLOR, Philip	1804	7-289
STEAR, John	1806	8- 88
STEEL, John	1730	1-250
John	1806	8- 99
STEELE, Ann	1839	17-416
STEEVER, Adam	1818	10-443
Adam	1827	12-336
Daniel	1818	10-507
STEIGER, Augustus	1840	17-483
Jacob	1821	11-212
John	1814	9-490
Mary	1823	11-620
STEINBECK, John C.	1821	11-209
STEINER, Bernard	1821	11-299
STEINMEYER, Margaret Elizabeth		
	1847	21-460
STEINNEFERD, Henry	1815	10-59
STEITZ, Michael	1789	4-364
may be Steltz		
STEMMENS, Richard	1829	13-303
STENSON, Martha	1844	20- 58
William	1826	12-305
STEPHENS, James	1802	7- 17
Joerge	1848	22-393
William	1794	5-153
STEPHENSON, Rachel	1804	7-280
Robert	1773	3-258
		& 359
STERETT, John	1787	4-194
Samuel		14-350
William	1787	4-256
STERQUEL, Peter	1846	21-305
STERRETT, Benj.	1824	12- 58
James	1796	5-435
Libby	1846	21-159
STEUART, James	1846	21- 71
Robert	1826	12-310
Robert G.	1849	23-287
STEVENS, Achsah	1844	20-170
George E.	1842	18-483
Rezin	1826	12-256
Robert	1846	21-105
William	1768	3- 92
STEVENSON, Ann	1806	8-105
Dr. Cosmo Gordon	1825	12-159
Edward	1760	2- 264

STEVENSON, Edward	1807	8-240	
Harriet Gore	1829	13-180	
Henry	1814	9-439	
Jemima	1810	8-467	
John	1785	4- 50	
		&v 52	
John	1786	4-147	
John	1831	13-500	
John W.	1845	20-461	
Joshua	1803	7-159	
Joshua	1823	11-600	
Josias	1832	14-146	
Mary	1820	11-162	
Nathan	1844	20- 97	
Richard	1815	10- 31	
Richard King	1777	3-337	
Samuel	1821	11-326	
Sater	1817	10-397	
STEVER, Elizabeth	1821	11-257	
STEWARD, John	1805	7-384	
STEWART, Archibald		14-345	
Benson	1838	16-432	
Charles	1802	6-482	
David	1817	10-356	
Eliza	1838	16-474	
James	1767	3- 76	
James	1831	14- 34	
John	1799	6-224	
John	1826	12-252	
John	1816	10-252	
Mary	1818	10-506	
Rachel	1816	10-192	
William	1842	19- 44	
STEYER, George	1786	4-157	
STIDGER, Harman	1805	8- 8	
George	1826	12-301	
STIGER, John	1814	9-490	
STILES, Philip	1811	9- 95	
William	1764	2-183	
STILLEY, John	1845	20-331	
STILTZ, Philip	1811	9- 95	
Rachel	1829	13-291	
		& 293	
STINCHCOMB, Action	1823	11-587	
Catherine	1791	4-553	
Christopher	1837	16-208	
Enoch	1826	12-284	
George	1827	12-397	
John	1779	3-382	
John	1807	8-163	

STINCHICOMB, John, Jr.	1828	13-121	
STINCHCOMB, McLane	1821	11-269	
Nathaniel	1806	8- 98	
Nelson	1839	17-211	
Ruth	1840	18- 60	
Thomas	1827	12-377	
Victor	1843	19-361	
STIRLING, Elizabeth	1843	19-362	
James	1820	11-145	
Jane	1834	14-481	
William	1832	14-267	
William	1838	17- 54	
STITCHER, Jacob	1800	6-335	
STITH, Drury	1850	23-430	
STOCK(S)DALE, John	1757	2-234	
John	1822	11-416	
See also Stocksdale.			
STOCKETT, Barbara	1817	10-313	
Henry	1808	8-319	
Joseph	1795	5-267	
Capt. William S.	1818	10-504	
STOCKSDALE, Edmund H.	1836	16- 47	
Edward	1779	3-376	
Edward	1809	8-401	
Nathan	1835	15-357	
STODDER, David	1806	8-101	
Marcia	1813	9-348	
STOKES, George	1741	1-386	
John	1732	1-257	
Robert	1756	2-110	
Susannah	1746	1-375	
STOLPP, Jacob	1846	21- 39	
STONDEHORF, Frederick	1800	6-343	
STONE, Elizabeth	1737	1-291	
John	1845	20-422	
William	1794	5-164	
William	1821	11-318	
STONEBRAKER, George	1843	19-330	
STORM, George	1813	9-375	
STORY, Mary	1846	21-194	
Rachel	1844	20-204	
Ralph	1783	3-534	
STOUFFER, Henry	1835	14-394	
STOUT, Lewis	1804	7-342	
STOUTSBURGOR, Andrew	1845	20-395	
STOVER, John	1774	3-278	
STOW, Thomas	1848	22-144	
STOXDALE, Edward	1779	3-376	
STRATTON, Robert	1836	16-124	
STRAWBRIDGE, Sarah	1699	1- 62	

STREBACH, George	1769	3-131
STREEBECK, Peter	1812	9-203
STREMMEL, Frederick	1807	8-247
STRICKER, John	1825	12-143
Mary	1830	13-495
STRIKE, Nicholas	1834	14-483
STROMBLE, Zachariah	1787	4-272
STRONG, James	1847	21-322
STROUBLE, Zachariah	1787	4-272
STRUTT, Peter	1843	19-338
STUART, James	1842	19- 77
Jane	1807	8-210
Michael	1849	23- 65
Richardson	1822	11-362
STULL, John	1802	8- 99
STUMP, William, Jr.	1821	11-236
SUBER, John	1835	15-303
SUBERS, Jane	1832	14-270
SUIRE, Edmond	1798	6-147
SULLIVAN, John	1848	22-432
SULTZER, Rudolph	1803	7-240
SUMMERS, Sarah	1802	7- 60
Wm. S.	1807	8-140
SUMMERWELL, Richard	1820	11-141
SUMNER, John	1758	2- 70
SUMWALT, Eliza	1835	15-328
George H.	1835	15-396
John	1847	21-481
Philip	1834	15-154
William Fletcher	1849	23-116
SUNDERLAND, John	1824	12- 78
SURE, Daniel	1804	7-289
SUTER, Charlotte	1849	23- 94
SUTLES, Charles	1828	13- 46
SUTHERLAND, St. Clair	1820	11-184
SUTTON, Alice	1808	8-337
Isaac	1811	9-171
Vincent	1843	19-365
SWAIN, Benj.	1844	20-210
SWAN, John	1821	11-284
Matthew	1830	13-470
SWANN, Edward	1712	1-120
SWARTZ, Peter	1822	11-440
SWARTZAUER, Philip	1811	9-191
SWARTZBAUGH, John	1828	13-36
SWEENEY, Thomas	1825	12- 92
		& 97
SWEENY, Elias	1806	8- 78
Geo. W.	1839	17-370
SWEETING, Edward	1809	8-417

SWEGGETT, James	1812	9-234
SWINDELL, Elizabeth	1705	1- 45
SWINYARD, John	1768	3- 91
SWITZER, John	1848	22-142
SWOOPE, Mary	1839	17-203
alias Polly Swope		
SYAR, Benjamin	1802	6-529
SYCKES, Mary	1819	11- 30
SYKES, John	1846	21-165
TABBS, Lucretia	1805	7-352
TAGART, Mary	1829	13-267
William	1802	7- 31
TAGG, Thomas	1847	22-115
		& 248
TAGGART, Henry	1824	12- 62
TAITTE, John	1798	6-128
TALBOT. See under Talbott.		
TALBOTT, Benj.	1816	10-108
Benj. Robinson	1788	4-309
Charles	1755	2-232
Edmund	1731	1-255
Edward	1797	6- 20
Lucy	1847	21-441
Stephen	1805	7-376
Temperance	1813	9-300
Thomas	1773	3-267
Thomas	1836	16-105
Vincent	1820	11- 92
William	1713	1-108
William	1752	2- 38
TALIAFERRO, George C.		
	1847	21-339
TANEY, Dorothy	1837	16-251
TANNOCH, James	1809	8-372
TAPLEY, Christopher	1682	1- 87
TASCHER, Marie F. C.		
	1839	17-347
TAYLOR, Abraham	1719	1-105
Abraham	1755	1-489
Bryan	1736	1-274
Edward	1829	13-308
George	1802	6-491
Henry	1785	4- 44
Hinemers H.	1802	7- 74
James	1835	15-339
James	1837	16-294
John	1676	1-113
John	1745	2-211

TAYLOR, John	1786	4-137	THERELL, Richard	1675	1- 3
John	1807	8-189	THERIAT, Augustus R.	1845	21-13
		& 190	THERRELL, Margaret	1677	1-110
John, Sr.	1822	11-430	THIMBLE, Joshua	1844	20- 21
Joseph	1789	4-346	See also Trimble, Joshua.		
See also pp. 348 and 363.			THOMAS, Angelus G. D.	1826	12-266
Joseph	1830	13-389	David	1720	1-168
Joseph	1846	21- 70	David	1746	1-363
Lawrence	1728	1-218	David	1769	3-109
Martha	1811	9- 97	David	1844	20-200
Mary	1843	19-398	Eleanor	1847	22- 63
Nicholas W.	1827	12-327	Evan	1827	12-380
Patience	1793	5-117	George	1847	22- 4
Richard	1729	2-187	Jeann	1825	12-180
Richard	1821	11-217	John	1803	7-185
Samuel	1845	20-429	John	1821	11-281
		& 462	John	1834	14-411
Sarah	1839	17-274	John	1842	19-102
Sarah	1843	19-448	Joseph	1748	1-392
Thomas	1825	12-197	Joseph	1848	22-206
Thomas	1834	15- 62	Luke	1816	10-100
Thomas V.	1837	16-327	Philip	1847	22- 61
William H.	1848	22-341	Thomas	1848	22-215
Vincent	1825	12-123	THOMPSON, Alexander	1843	19-407
William H.	1848	22-341	Andrew	1739	1-310
William M.	1833	14-394	Andrew	1761	2-329
William M.	1841	18-401	Andrew	1813	9-357
William W.	1832	14-206	George C.	1830	13-385
TAYMAN, Benjamin	1731	1-251	Hugh	1826	12-308
Sarah	1745	2-217	James	1837	16-359
TCHUDY. See Tschudy.			James	1839	17-277
TEAGUE, Daniel	1809	8-435	James W.	1844	20-167
TEAL, Edward	1720	1-158	Jane	1830	13-455
John	1722	1-188	John	1800	6-253
TEEL, Anson B.	1845	20-359	John	1813	9-340
TEMPER, Conrad	1826	12-295	John	1816	10-190
TEMPLE, Miles	1705	1- 62	John H.	1845	20-334
Thomas	1710	1- 33	Martha E.	1843	19-347
TENANT, Thomas	1836	15-442	Moses	1798	6-132
		& 448	Rachel	1781	3-439
TENSFIELD, Margaret	1832	14-252	Richard	1698	1-136
TENTER, John	1773	3-243	Robert	1800	6-307
TERRY, Sarah	1816	10-189	Samuel	1838	17- 58
William	1811	9-170	Sarah	1823	11-514
TESSIER, John	1841	18-275	Sarah	1829	13-282
TEVIS, Benj.	1802	7- 84			& 376
Robert, Sr.	1796	5-475	Thomas	1822	11-379
THARPE, Thomas	1802	6-484	Thomas	1834	15-293
THEOBALD, Jennett	1831	14- 56	William	1810	8-498
John	1813	9-313	William	1833	14-359

THOMPSON, William	1847	22- 94		TOON, Samuel	1808	8-320
THOMSON, Allen	1849	23- 11		TOPKIN, Gerard	1818	10-533
John	1802	7 26		TORRANCE, Charles	1822	11-444
Lawrence	1819	10-613		Elizabeth	1829	13-218
THORNBURGH, Isabella	1838	17-125		TOWELL, Zacharias	1832	14-120
Joseph	1820	11-107		TOWERS, Eliza	1822	11-491
Roland	1702	1- 81		James	1813	9-345
THORNTON, William	1769	3-116		TOWNSEND, Joseph	1841	18-373
THORP, Agnes	1831	14- 62		TOWSON, Dinah	1783	3-532
THORPE, Thomas	1802	6-484		Joseph	1745	2-218
THWAITES, Geo.	1816	10-227		Susanna	1811	9-116
listed as Trivaites.				William, Jr.	1768	3- 96
TIBBS, William	1732	1-262		William	1772	3-222
TIBOR, Susannah	1820	11-125		TOY, Frances	1836	16- 43
TIENCKEN, John	1834	14-444		Isaac N.	1834	15-158
TIERNAN, Ann	1841	18-212		TRABAND, George	1848	22-371
Luke	1839	17-409		TRACEY, John	1842	19- 85
Michael	1837	16-235		Mary	1824	12- 57
TILLYARD, John	1686	1- 55		TRACY, Garret W.	1849	23-163
TILOR, Susannah	1820	11-125		John	1795	5-289
TILTON, James	1841	18-339		Nicholas	1849	23- 99
TILYARD, William	1806	8- 80		Susannah B.	1833	14-357
alias Thomas F. W.				TRAVERSE, Plan	1835	15-234
TIMBRELL, Joseph	1794	5-186		may be Flan.		
TIMMS, John	1811	9- 87		TRAYNOR, Thomas	1783	3-490
TINKER, William	1801	6-468		TREANOR, Ann	1835	15-358
TINNEY, Edward	1785	4- 59		TREDWAY, John	1767	3- 64
TIPTON, Aquilla	1827	13- 10		Thomas	1749	1-469
Samuel	1804	7-334		TRIMBLE, Isaac	1824	12- 8
Susannah	1843	19-237		John, of Wm.	1847	22-103
William	1726	1-228		Joshua	1844	20- 21
William	1797	5-509		see also Thimble.		
TODD, Bernard	1816	10-221		William	1819	10-611
Thomas	1677	1- 1		William	1830	13-493
Thomas, Jr.	1715	1-227		William H.	1848	22-487
		& 230		TRIPOLET, Mary Magdalen	1791	5- 24
Thomas	1739	1-304		See also pp. 29 and 38.		
William	1813	9-383		TRIVAITES. See Thwaites.		
William	1813	9-383		TROTER, Elizabeth	1766	3- 44
TOLLEY, James	1744	2- 14		TROTTEN, Luke	1752	1-314
Martha	1802	6-478		TROTTON, Susanna	1795	5-322
Mary	1733	2-199		TROUP, Elizabeth	1844	20-192
Mary	1744	2- 21		TROYER, George	1786	4-144
Susanna	1833	13-416		George	1825	12- 95
		& 417		TRUMP, William B.	1847	21-417
Thomas	1732	1-263		TSCHUDY, John, Sr.	1799	6-214
Thomas, Jr.	1734	2-197		Martin	1828	13-127
Walter	1783	3-507		Mary M.	1833	14-336
TOMLINSON, John	1829	13-266		Nicholas	1810	9- 6
TOOLE, Thomas	1818	10-546		Winbert	1786	4-193
		& 547		TUCKER, Elizabeth C.	1842	19- 72

INDEX OF BALTIMORE COUNTY WILLS

TUCKER, Samuel	1838	16-528	
Thomas	1849	23-272	
		& 309	
William A.	1849	23- 74	
TUCKEY, Elisha	1846	21- 83	
TUCKWORTH, Robert	1818	10-501	
TUFTS, Timothy	1809	8-431	
TULL, Bridget	1806	8- 72	
Elijah	1784	3-593	
TULLY, Edward	1782	3-464	
TUNSTIL, Henry	1790	4-506	
TUREL, John M. B.	1836	16- 39	
TURNBULL, Andrew	1813	9-342	
Elizabeth	1841	18-315	
Sarah	1811	9-184	
TURNER, Elisha	1843	19-298	
John	1849	23-140	
Joshua	1841	18-308	
Margaret	1839	17-303	
Martha	1836	15-492	
Mary	1840	18- 54	
Michael	1833	14-372	
		& 373	
Robert	1837	16-281	
Thomas	1836	15-441	
TURNPAUGH, Christopher	1805	7-430	
		& 433	
TURPIN, Mary	1846	21-266	
TYE, George	1813	9-333	
John	1739	1-321	
TYPTON, See Tipton.			
TYRELL, James	1827	12-413	
TYSON, Elisha	1824	11-643	
George, Jr.	1837	16-409	
Hannah	1822	11-388	
Isaac	1784	3-566	
Jacob	1835	15-353	
Mary	1843	19-323	
UHLER, Erasmus	1814	9-481	
George	1818	10-411	
ULERICK, Michael	1819	11- 74	
UNDERWOOD, Elihu	1804	7-318	
Mary	1806	8- 55	
Samuel	1746	1-375	
William	1800	6-246	
UNVERZAGT, Tobias	1844	20-119	
UPDEGRAFF, Hannah	1847	22- 5	
UPPERCO, Jacob	1794	5-157	

UPPERCO, Jacob, Jr.	1795	5-339	
URIE, James	1826	12-300	
URIL, Robert	1801	6-392	
USHER, Abraham	1795	5-325	
James	1801	6-469	
Mary	1840	18-128	
Thomas	1786	4-126	
UTIE, George	1678	1- 59	
VALENTINE, Geo.	1806	8- 42	
VAN BIBBER, Abraham	1805	7-436	
Isaac	1825	12-125	
		& 126	
VAN BRUN, Ann de L.	1837	16-247	
VANCE, William	1816	10-182	
VAN DEAVER, Jane	1730	1-241	
VAN HORNE, Benjamin	1771	3-186	
VAN PRADELLAS, Cassandra Deye			
	1815	10- 39	
VAN RANST, Rebecca	1810	8-497	
VANSANT, William W.	1850	23-405	
VANSILL, John J. L.	1795	5-247	
VANWYCK, Elizabeth	1820	11- 94	
VEALE, Nicholas	1797	6- 43	
Pearce	1797	6- 45	
VEAZEY, Edward Henry	1839	17-226	
VENABLE, Sally	1841	18-196	
VENABLES, Milcha	1841	18-262	
VANANCOURT, Jules De	1836	16- 92	
VETHAKE, Frederick	1808	8-309	
VETREE, Mary	1826	12-224	
VICKERS, Agness	1848	22-356	
Amos	1800	6-287	
VICKERY, Stephen	1809	8-440	
Thomas	1810	8-474	
VICKORY, John	1711	1-119	
VICTOR, John Augustus	1846	21-108	
VICTORY, Daniel	1845	20-264	
VILLARD, Martha	1818	10-512	
VINCENT, Samuel	1825	12-179	
VINE, Roland	1746	1-373	
VINSON, James	1822	11-480	
VINTERS, James	1766	3- 54	
VOIRY, Charles	1807	8-189	
VOLUMBRUM, Jeanne	1832	14-212	
VONEIFF, John	1842	19- 17	
VON KAPFF, Bernard John			
	1828	13- 22	
Jane C.	1840	18-142	

INDEX OF BALTIMORE COUNTY WILLS

VUYTON, Pierre	1794	5=454
WADDELL, Francis	1823	11-518
WADE, Emanuel	1845	20-442
Henry	1775	3-313
John	1791	5- 20
WAGNER, Peter	1848	22-422
WAGONER, Philip	1840	17-484
WAKEMAN, Edward	1753	2-251
WALKER, Charles	1825	12-196
Charles	1834	14-429
Charlotte	1843	19-477
Elizabeth Hulse	1830	13-354
George	1743	1-341
George	1833	14-370
Henry	1799	6-163
James	1820	11-172
Joseph	1800	6-263
Lewis	1811	9-190
Lucy	1820	11-179
Mary	1839	17-279
Prudence	1841	18-260
Samuel D.	1848	22-359
Susanna	1822	11-425
Thomas	1802	7- 22
Thomas	1818	10-520
William Cradock	1830	13-470
WALL, John	1806	8- 73
Mary	1831	13-497
WALLACE, Alexander	1844	20- 49
John	1788	4-295
Joseph	1821	11-222
Margaret	1849	23- 47
Samuel	1754	2- 60
WALLAR, William	1801	6-436
See also Walters, William.		
WALLER, Basil	1805	7-389
William	1749	1-464
William	1830	13-365
WALLEY, Zedekiah	1783	3-502
WALN, Nicholas	1824	12- 65
WALRAVEN, John	1814	9-429
WALSH, Edward	1795	5-259
Jane	1835	15-310
John	1817	10-373
Michael	1800	6-298
Richard	1847	21-379
WALTER, Jacob	1830	13-420
Margaret	1830	13-478
Maria	1829	13-264

WALTER, Peter	1830	13-461
Philip	1819	10-588
William	1801	6-436
See William Wallar.		
WALTERS, Alexander	1822	11-426
Ariana	1798	6- 93
Eleanor	1814	9-398
Job	1843	19-388
Joseph	1838	17-165
Philip	1798	6-137
See also Philip Waters.		
Rebecca	1837	16-329
Suzette	1837	16-325 & 328
William	1835	15-363
WALTHAM, John	1822	11-414
Thomas	1815	10- 12
WALTHOM, Thomas	1816	10-156
WANN, Edward	1792	5- 73
John	1784	4- 17
WANTZ, Adam	1815	9-529
WARD, Edward	1730	1-247
Edward	1799	6-255
Edward	1840	3- 18
Eliza	1836	16- 63
Elizabeth	1824	11-636
George	1818	10-525
John	1829	13-258
John B.	1833	14-297
Joseph	1754	2- 50
Mary	1828	13- 14
Mary A.	1783	3-547
Patrick	1832	14-157
Samuel	1731	1-257
Sophia	1809	8-371
William	1844	20- 87
WARFIELD, Anderson	1828	13- 40
David	1821	11-290
Dennis	1806	8-112
Elijah	1814	9-449
Susanna	1812	9-229
WARHEIM, Catherine	1813	9-292
WARNER, Catherine	1846	21-110
Frederick	1817	10-294
George	1829	13-224
Jacob	1813	9-341
Margaret	1807	8-267
Margaret	1837	16-403
Mary	1823	11-567
Michael	1848	22-306
Philip	1811	9-127

WARNER, Susan	1846	21-120
WARNICK, Sarah	1840	17-486
WARNKEN, Rachel	1821	11-292
WARRENTON, William	1797	6- 48
WARTMAN, Abraham	1839	17-242
Dorothy	1845	20-317
WASHINGTON, Wm. Augustine	1811	9-106
WASTMAN, Jordan Nicholas (or John N.)	1796	5-408
WATERHOUSE, Ann	1841	18-455
William	1807	8-243
WATERS, Charles	1846	21-171 & 199
Edward	1810	9- 68
Eliza	1796	5-378
Joseph	1845	20-480
Mary	1800	6- 0
Philip	1798	6-137
See also Philip Walters.		
WATERTON, John	1682	1- 69
WATKINS, Gassaway	1840	18-112
John	1847	21-464
Samuel	1743	1-349
Samuel	1795	5-336
Samuel	1816	10-212
William	1754	2- 61
William, Sr.	1839	17-176
WATSON, Lancelot	1762	2-141
Robert	1821	11-272
Sarah, Sr.	1843	19-394
William	1784	3-558
William	1844	20-137 & 211
WATTERS, Godfrey	1754	2- 51
WATT, James P.	1833	14-387
WATTS, Ezekiel	1818	10-408
Nathaniel	1848	22-411
Robert	1842	19- 21
Sarah	1803	7-149
Sarah	1809	8-462
Thomas	1837	16-282
WAYBILL, Mary	1836	16- 46
WEAR, Elizabeth	1823	11-612
William	1802	7- 71
WERHAM, Henry	1812	9-248
WEATHERBURN, John	1811	9-121
Sally	1843	19-213
WEATHERBY, Wm.	1811	9-193
WEAVER, Caspar	1811	9- 94

WEAVER, Casper	1829	13-179
Daniel	1797	5-512
George	1831	14- 72
George E.	1848	22-304
Jacob	1814	9-497
John	1792	5- 48
John	1799	6-205
John	1803	7-238
Susanna	1815	10- 97
WEBB, Charles	1849	23- 69
Henry	1819	10-584
Mary	1775	3-312
Nelly	1846	21-301
WEBER, Henry	1847	21-425
WEBSTER, Eliza	1788	4-325
Isaac	1759	1-473
James	1802	7- 50
John, Jr.	1721	1-506
John	1753	2-248
John, of Michael	1761	2-332
Michael	1764	2-176
WEDERSTRANDT, Mary Blake	1846	21-277
WEDGE, Susanna	1825	12-198
WEEMS, Augusta M.	1837	16-243
WEER, Thomas	1802	7-142
William	1804	7-312
WEHRLY, Jonathan	1848	22-285
William T.	1849	23-218
WEIMAN, Barnet	1815	10- 32
WEIPLING, Michael	1820	11-105
WEIR, Charles	1806	8- 90 & 95
WEIS, Michael	1806	8- 79
WEISE, Augustus	1817	10-381
Barbara	1840	18- 19
Martin	1797	6- 25
See also Martin Welsh.		
WEITER, Susanna	1811	9-195
WELCH, Laban	1843	19-360
Margaret	1834	15-201
Martico Merryman	1832	14-192
Pierce	1722	1-193
William	1802	7- 47
WELD, Martha	1847	21-456
WELFORD, Richard C.	1844	20-193
WELLER, Geo.	1820	11-131
WELLHAM, Ann	1825	12-195
WELLMORE, William	1830	13-440
WELLS, Benjamin	1801	6-470

WELLS, Benjamin	1830	13-448	WHEELER, Benjamin	1849	23-275
Blanche	1704	1- 95	Edward	1836	16-149
Charles	1741	1-382	Jacob	1799	6-191
Cyprian	1814	9=423	James	1834	14-452
George	1695	1-200	Jane	1843	19-321
George	1783	3-578	John	1821	11-215
John Francis	1837	16-427	Jonathan	1816	10-131
Margaret	1826	12-312	Joseph	1828	13-153
Mary	1823	11-562	Joseph S.	1828	13- 19
Mary	1850	23-348	Leonard	1747	1-405
Nathan	1756	2-113	Martha	1828	13- 80
Nelson	1843	19-266	Michael F.	1832	14-179
Thomas	1846	21-179	Nathan	1797	6- 35
William	1778	3-361	Nathan	1838	16-527
WELLMORE, Peter G.	1815	10- 16	Richard	1808	8-307
WELSH, Adam	1841	18-252	Samuel	1771	3-179
Edward	1713	1-124	Solomon	1787	4-204
Henry	1837	16-205	Thomas	1770	3-171
John	1786	4-165	William	1738	1-299
John	1796	5-419	William	1767	3- 75
Martin	1797	6- 25	William	1808	8-283
See also Weise, Martin.			William	1825	12-128
WELTY, Andrew	1772	3-221	William S.	1795	5-242
WEST, Cassandra	1825	12-120	WHELAN, John	1844	20- 42
Isaac	1847	21-437			& 139
James	1812	9-246	WHEYLAND, Thomas	1820	11-121
John, of B.	1848	22-159	WHIFFING, James	1837	16-302
Robert	1748	1-408	WHIPPER, Isaac	1848	22-402
Stephen	1790	4-401	WHIPS, Benjamin	1757	2-233
Thomas	1768	3- 87	Margaret	1764	2-187
Rev. William	1791	4-541	WHITE, Abraham	1835	15-367
William	1795	5-309	Elizabeth	1832	14-268
WESTALL, George	1718	1-127	Euphemia	1810	8-501
WESTAR, Richard	1788	4-433	George	1816	10-137
WESTERMAN, Joshua	1842	19-155	Hugh	1844	19-486
William	1832	14-193	James	1783	3-581
WESTROME, Andrew	1811	9-152	James	1843	19-208
WETHERALL, Henry	1738	1-301	Job	1837	16-270
WETHERED, Mary	1832	14-239	John	1821	11-298
WEVER, Philip	1821	11-268	John Campbell	1848	22-265
WHALAND, Thomas	1803	7-155	Luke	1797	5-493
WHEATLY, Elizabeth	1808	8-343	Margaret	1821	11-267
WHEEDEN, Thomas	1840	18- 32	Nicholas	1831	14- 46
WHEELER, Alice	1840	17-497	Oliver	1799	6-197
Ann	1832	14-160	Stevenson	1826	12-260
Archibald	1843	19-358	Thomas	1799	6-188
Benjamin	1741	1-388	Thomas	1816	10-233
Benjamin	1770	3-174	Thomas	1828	13- 14
Benjamin	1807	8-215	WHITECOMB, Sarah	1757	2-235
Benjamin	1847	21-386	WHITEFORD, Michael	1762	2-133

WHITEHEAD, Francis	1722	1-191	WILL, Mary	1849	23- 55
Nathan	1773	3-247	WILLARD, Julius	1844	20- 79
Shepherd	1796	5-399	Salem	1821	11-311
Thomas	1808	8-290	WILLDAY, Edward	1710	1- 78
WHITER, John	1786	4-145	WILLIAMS, Baruch	1818	10-424
		& 147	Charles	1833	14-367
WHITFIELD, James	1834	15-133	Dutton	1814	9-455
WHITING, Wm. B.	1839	17-365	Edw. Green	1829	13-192
WIBBING, Jacob	1819	10-605	Elizabeth	1839	17-212
May be Wibling.			Ellen	1848	22-357
WICKERD, John	1832	14-139	Henry Lee	1826	12-279
WICKHAM, John	1847	21-398	Jacob	1827	12-424
Margaret	1848	22-400	James R.	1849	23-253
Peter	1834	15- 60			& 353
WIER, John M.	1849	23-309	James R. A.	1850	23-449
		& 399	Jeremiah	1815	10- 77
WIESENTHAL, Andrew	1798	6-145	John	1799	6-231
WIGART, Andrew	1842	19- 57	John	1836	16- 86
George, Jr.	1840	17-496	John	1836	16-210
WIGLEY, Edward	1795	5-328	Joseph	1822	11-432
WIGHT, Rezin	1842	18-474	Lewis	1829	13-161
Richard	1809	8-370	Lydia	1812	9-246
WIGNALL, James	1814	9-430	Mary	1789	4-392
WILBOURNE, Edward	1730	1-249	Matthew	1821	11-331
WILCOX, William	1805	7-377	Otho Holland	1794	5-180
WILD, Lewis	1832	14-114	Richard	1767	3- 57
WILDERMAN, Jacob, Sr.	1787	4-236	Richard	1823	11-560
WILES, James	1838	16-488	Robert	1820	11-203
William	1842	18-481	Robert	1821	11-232
WILEY, John	1777	3-340	Samuel, Jr.	1847	21-438
WILHELM, Henry	1798	6- 92	Sarah	1847	21-388
Henry	1843	19-373	Spindello	1849	23-281
John, Sr.	1849	23-135	Thomas	1850	23-429
WILKENSON, Daniel	1820	11-120	William	1837	16-385
WILKERSON, David	1820	11-120	WILLIAMSON, Adolphus	1845	20-358
Sarah	1834	14-406	Alexander	1805	7-390
WILKES, James	1838	16-488	David	1831	14- 1
WILKINS, Henry	1847	21-453	David	1839	17-219
Joseph	1850	23-481	John	1844	20-201
William	1823	11-611	Joseph	1843	19-403
William	1832	14-237	Thomas	1789	4-379
WILKINSON, Charles	1819	11- 72			& 384
Daniel	1820	11-120	WILLIARD, Benj.	1803	7-224
James	1842	19-126	WILLIS, Ann	1842	8- 19
Richard	1833	14-364	William	1782	3-470
Robert	1760	2-275	WILLISON, Liddy	1829	13-185
Samuel	1802	7-117	WILLMOTT, Sarah	1838	16-459
Stephen	1778	3-363	WILLOT, Amade de F.	1828	13- 93
William	1718	1-131	WILLSON, Hugh	1802	6-547
William	1783	3-542	William	1790	4-393
William	1789	4-323	WILMOTT, John	1783	3-550

WILMOTT, John	1719	1- 84 & 153	WILSON, William	1834	14-479
John	1748	1-418	William	1836	16-111
John	1783	3-550	WIMSET, Ann	1841	18-32?
Rachel	1761	2-348	WINCHESTER, David	1835	15-342
Robert	1773	3-265	Elizabeth	1847	22- 81
William	1783	3-547	Hannah	1831	14- 55
WILSON, Andrew	1830	13-342	Lydia	1849	23- 91
Benj.	1815	10- 41	William	1812	9-235
Benj.	1833	14-389	William	1822	11-494
Benkid	1781	3-443	WINDER, Araminta	1845	20-254 & 426
David	1836	15-476			
Felix	1849	23-308	Levin	1819	11- 31
Henry	1799	6-234	William H.	1824	12- 37
Henry	1816	10-160	William Sinday	1844	20- 15
Isaac	1827	12-374	WINEMAN, Ann Barbara	1811	9-112
Jacob	1797	6- 39	Henry	1811	9- 85
James	1770	3-177	WING, Peter	1784	3-558
James	1802	7- 70	WINGATE, Susannah	1826	12-222
James	1844	20- 29	WINN, John	1831	14-104
Jane	1819	11- 20	Richard	1758	2- 86
John	1783	3-541	William T.	1848	22-249
John	1807	8-152	See also pp. 320 and 385.		
John	1827	12-366	WINNING, John	1789	4-369
John	1830	13-450	Margaret	1794	5-144
John	1837	16-253	WINSLOW, John	1803	7-168
John	1837	16-259	WINTER, Ralph	1713	1-108
John	1843	19-461	WINTKLE, Elizabeth	1833	14-390
John	1846	21-233	James	1810	9- 15
John Kidd	1835	15-417	WIREMAN, Christian.		
Joseph of Joseph	1812	9-272	See Wiseman, Christian.		
Joseph	1822	11-394	WIRGMAN, Peter	1819	11- 43
Lydia	1839	17-272	WIRT, William	1834	14-462
Lydia	1846	21-114	WISE, John, Sr.	1832	14-155
Margaret R.	1829	13-189	WISEMAN, Christian	1800	6-265
Margaretta	1840	17-488	WISNER, Carahabuck	1832	14-343
Mary	1842	19-119	May be Kerrenhappuck.		
Mary P.	1843	19-452	Elizabeth	1815	10- 75
Michael	1843	19-454	George	1831	14- 95
Nicholas	1836	16- 77	Matthias, Jr.	1812	9-223
Robert	1844	20-221	Mathias	1823	11-529
Ruth R.	1826	12-231	Sarah	1834	15- 75
Sarah Maria	1831	14- 95	WISTER, Richard	1788	4-433
Thomas	1845	20-266	WITH, George	1751	3-416
William	1753	2-253	WITTICAR, John	1713	1-106
William	1768	3- 97	WOLDMAN, John H. H.	1849	23- 57
William	1805	7-377	WOLF, Elizabeth	1823	11-53?
William	1824	12- 19	Jacob	1817	10-331
William	1825	12- 93	Valentine	1820	11-135
William	1829	13-256	WOLFF, John Michael	1778	3-371
			WOLLEN, Zacharia	1837	16-310

WOLIRY, Margaret	1829	13-216	
		& 369	
WOLSEY, Catherine	1797	6- 61	
WONN, Edward	1792	5- 73	
William Welsh	1826	12-317	
WOOD, Barbara	1800	6-262	
Barbara	1833	14-368	
James	1802	7- 53	
John Rigby	1801	6-438	
Joshua	1749	1-460	
Leonard	1818	10-472	
Sarah	1849	23-107	
William	1736	1-281	
William	1769	3-114	
William, Jr.	1798	6-143	
See also Woods.			
WOODALL, Ralph	1734	2-196	
WOODCOCK, Robert	1810	9- 75	
WOODEN, Benjamin, Jr.	1847	22-134	
Francis	1811	9-177	
John	1769	3-123	
John, Sr.	1790	4-425	
		& 431	
John	1823	11-593	
Rachel, Sr.	1797	5-537	
Rachel	1823	11-600	
Solomon	1794	5-161	
Stephen Gill	1829	13-182	
Thomas	1833	14-331	
William	1761	2-336	
WOODLAND, Blackledge	1770	3-250	
WOODS, Cautil	1841	18-172	
May be Caryil.			
James	1795	5-331	
John	1832	14-115	
William	1826	12-298	
See also Wood.			
WOODWARD, Jane	1775	3-303	
John	1782	3-468	
Mary	1789	4-352	
Thomas	1744	2- 17	
William	1774	3-282	
William Garrett	1799	6-208	
WOODYEAR, Edw. G.	1832	14-194	
WOOLBUD, George	1834	15- 78	
WOOLF, James	1836	15-495	
WOOLFOLK, Austin	1847	21-382	
WOOLFORD, Cassandra	1847	22- 27	
WOOLLEN, Robison	1849	22-492	
Thomas	1829	13-327	

WOOLSEY, John	1788	4-311
WORKMAN, Hugh	1786	4-129
WORRELL, Henry, Jr.	1782	3-473
Thomas	1806	8- 74
		& 88
WORTHINGTON, Abby	1821	11-280
Charles	1847	22- 28
Hannah	1796	5-447
John T.	1834	15-110
John T. H.	1849	23-102
Marcella	1842	19- 68
Martha	1832	14-131
Mary	1776	3-303
Samuel	1811	9-200
Samuel	1815	10- 20
Thomas	1821	11-238
Thomas	1821	11-253
Thomas	1834	14-441
Vachel	1833	14-279
William	1825	12-184
WOSTLER, Ulerick	1761	2-346
WOULDS, Alice	1826	12-228
WREN, Joseph	1832	14-166
William	1795	5-327
WRESHLER, Morrice	1779	3-387
WRIGHT, Bloyce	1737	1-287
Francis	1666	1- 57
Isaac	1746	1-352
Jacob	1770	3-170
John	1744	2- 20
John	1834	15- 66
John	1836	16- 21
John	1845	20-468
Joseph	1828	13- 99
Malcolm	1830	13-352
Solomon	1829	13-251
Solomon	1848	22-164
Stephen C.	1839	17-248
William	1724	1-207
William	1740	1-326
William	1779	4-555
WRIOTHESLY, Henry	1709	3-321
WYANT, Anna Maria	1824	12- 54
Anna Mary	1827	12-331
Peter	1817	10-373
WYLE, Athaliah	1828	13- 35
WYMBS, James	1825	12-185
WYSE, William	1814	9-440
WYSHAM, Ezekiel C.	1850	23-472

Other Heritage Books by Robert W. Barnes
and Bettie Stirling Carothers

1783 Tax List of Baltimore County

Index of Baltimore County Wills, 1659–1850

Other Heritage Books by Robert W. Barnes:

Baltimore and Fell's Point Directory of 1796

Baltimore County, Marriage References, 1659–1746

Baltimore County, Maryland Deed Abstracts, 1659–1750

Gleanings from Maryland Newspapers, 1776–85

Gleanings from Maryland Newspapers, 1786–90

Gleanings from Maryland Newspapers, 1791–95

Index to Marriages and Deaths in the
Baltimore County Advocate, 1850–1864

Other Heritage Books by Bettie Stirling Carothers:

1776 Census of Maryland

1783 Tax List of Maryland, Part I:
Cecil, Talbot, Harford and Calvert Counties

Maryland Oaths of Fidelity

Maryland Source Records: Volume 1

www.ingramcontent.com/pod-product-compliance
Lightning Source LLC
Chambersburg PA
CBHW062107090426
42741CB00015B/3354